MAINLY FOR WOMEN

Shows how a greater awareness of yours and your partner's body can increase your capacity for physical enjoyment and personal fulfilment.

GW01072167

MAINLY FOR WOMEN

A Guide to Love-making

by

ROBERT CHARTHAM

THORSONS PUBLISHERS LIMITED
Wellingborough, Northamptonshire

First Trade Paperback Edition
(revised and reset) 1983
Second Impression 1984

British Library Cataloguing in Publication Data

Chartham, Robert
    Mainly for women: a guide to love-making.
    1. Sex instruction for women
    I. Title
    306.7'024042   HQ46

    ISBN 0-7225-0800-X

Printed and bound in Great Britain

Contents

Foreword

by
A General Practitioner

The author of this book has written on a difficult subject in a direct manner, honestly and without shame.

We all know, I suppose, that many partnerships are made unhappy because of sexual difficulties between man and woman, and there is strong evidence for believing that faulty sexual relationships may, and too often do, lead to unfaithfulness and broken partnerships – a point of which the author is acutely aware. Unless one has first-hand experience of it, it is almost impossible to appreciate the degree of ignorance, and the fear of practical sex, that is encountered in clinics where young women attend for advice and help.

Many of these young women have never enjoyed normal intercourse, some, no form of intercourse at all. Until they have plucked up the courage to visit the clinic to seek advice, they have tolerated this situation because either they have had no sex instruction in early years or the sex instruction they were given was faulty; or other women have told them that 'sex' is just something for men to enjoy.

Learning to love is a process of which sexual knowledge and

experience are a part. Since a woman is a partner in a love-relationship it is wrong to deprive her of her share of sexual pleasure which should be derived from the sexual side of love.

Young women and men, and even couples who have been married for many years, could read this book without fear or shame. The author's approach is morally sound, and he attempts to provide a true and honest guide.

Many of us will be glad of this guide to practical love-making.

Introduction

Divorce Court judges, doctors, psychiatrists and marriage-counsellors know only too well how often sexual difficulties can wreck a marriage or partnership between a man and a woman.

The great tragedy is that ninety per cent of these difficulties need never have arisen if one, or both of the partners had had any practical knowledge of the sex functions beyond a little rudimentary love-making and how orgasm in intercourse is achieved in the simplest way.

The truth of the implication of this statement – that English men and women are not very skilled in the art of practical love-making – may at first seem doubtful. In this second half of the twentieth century the general attitude towards sex is one of increasing frankness and there are readily available today such a large number of books designed to help couples to understand and overcome the sexual difficulites they may encounter, should they be unable to avoid them altogether, that one would think that men and women should be as well versed in sex as they are in the other aspects of living. Indeed, one might reasonably expect couples who are not happy in their sex relations to be in a tiny minority, judging by the tens of thousands of books about sex that are sold every year.

Unfortunately this is not so, as the divorce statistics show, and the reason, I believe, is to be found in two typical answers – one by a man: 'Oh, but I know what to do! I've read such and such books about it'; the other by a woman: 'I've read so and so, but it did not tell me much; and anyway, that's the man's responsibility, isn't it?'

A study of quite a large number of books reveals that many of their writers, including even Dr Marie Stopes, have not realized that the majority of average men, imaginative though they may be in other directions, when it comes to the practice of sex show an abysmal lack of imagination. The failure to appreciate this has led the writers of generally helpful books to fall short of what is really necessary when they come to describing the actual technique of love-making. They have tried to put over what they want to say by hints and implication, when actually what is needed are simple and frank stage-by-stage descriptions and explanations.

John Smith is capable of reading and understanding what he reads, but his imagination does not take him all the way along the path upon which the writers have set him and then left him to find the rest of the way himself. He is not held back by the lack of the spirit of adventure, it is just that he does not know in which direction adventure lies.

Joan Smith finds even less guidanace in these books, because it is just not there for her, and the absence of it fits in with her preconceived notion that it is 'up to the man'. If only she knew that her man is only a very little way ahead of her and that this notion she has of his responsibility is one of the causes of her later difficulties, I am quite sure she would not be content.

It is because I am quite convinced that if only couples knew where to go they would go there that I have decided to set out a clearly sign-posted route.

To make quite sure that men shall not have the chance of shrugging it off with a mutter 'Just another book on sex', I am taking the woman into my confidence and making her the guide.

Now, I want to stress as strongly as I possibly can that I am dealing in this book with only *one* of the many aspects of sex – the actual practice of physical love-making. I am doing so because it is in the practice of sex as an expression of love – that is, excluding the procreative aspects – that couples most often come a cropper. For this reason, too, I have been as full in my descriptions of techniques and their accompanying explanations as to why such and such a thing can happen if such and such a thing is done as it seemed to me would be useful at this stage, which is really transitional between the old theories of education for practical sex and what I believe should be the true aim of such education.

This approach of mine, which I have tried to keep as simple as possible by excluding most of the other aspects of sex, may give to many readers the impression that I regard physical sex as the most important aspect of our sex lives. I want to make it absolutely clear, therefore, that this is not my view.

I regard sex first and foremost as the visible physical means by which a couple can express their emotional love for one another. Love in all its implications is extremely difficult to describe – if, in fact, it can be described at all satisfactorily; but even so, I am sure that you do not need me to tell you that it is upon love that the family and the home are founded. Love for a marriage partner can be expressed in any number of ways, and yet I do not think that I shall be contradicted when I say that the great majority of couples find a need for one special way in which they can demonstrate to one another their deep love in a manner which cannot possibly be misunderstood.

It is because love is, on the whole, abstract, an emotion, something that is felt and so can only be seen by transferring the results of its influence to other things, that this need for visible expression exists. It is because deep and real love of a man for a woman and of a woman for a man is usually felt only for one person that it is something very special and very intimate. It is because of this intimacy that the need is felt to express this love in the most intimate way possible; and the most intimate visible expression is the sharing of bodies, just as emotional love in its fullest sense must include the sharing of minds. It is because the fullest physical sharing of bodies is only achieved in love-making that sex and love are complements of one another, and that sex plays an extremely important role in the experience of a full life.

But it is not only in the mutual love-relationship of man and woman that sex plays this important role. It is the basis of the family, for without sex there can be no children.

The family is an extension of the love of husband and wife. It broadens the horizons of love, entails a further sharing; and though it is brought into being by the operation of sex, it gives rise to a new kind of love, a sexless love, which is as important in the full development of character, personality and being as the sexually-based love of husband and wife.

But the mother-instinct cannot be fulfilled without the operation of sex, and for this reason sex for a woman has a deeper significance than it has for a man. For while it is true that a father-instinct motivates a man to produce children, his instinct rests on a different foundation from that on which the woman's mother-instinct rests.

When a woman becomes pregnant she carries her child within her for several months, feeding it from her bloodstream and making it actually part of her. After it is born she feeds it and tends it, and for many months it relies solely on her. In these circumstances it would be strange indeed if a very special relationship did not exist between them.

The father's part in the conception of this child is completed in a fleeting moment. His reaction to fatherhood has its basis in pride, and though he loves his child, this love is really a reflection, in part, of the love he has for its mother.

Because of these different reactions to parenthood the attitude of a woman towards the procreative function of sex is to bestow a greater significance on the sex-act. For her, apart from its being the expression of her love for her partner, its physical aspects are, generally speaking, less important to her than its procreative function; while for her partner, the procreative function is subordinate to the physical experience.

This being so, speaking broadly, the woman's interest in physical love can be less than her partner's, and this produces a different approach to the sex-act by man and woman.

Despite this, however, women who truly love their partners do appreciate fully how the sex-act can be used and should be used as an expression of love. But apart from this, women who have experienced physical sexual satisfaction know that this satisfaction produces relief from physical and mental tensions which in turn produces physical and mental well-being in whose atmosphere love may flourish far more luxuriantly than it would do if the sensations of well-being did not exist.

The indulgence of physical love is, therefore, as important to a woman as it is to a man, both for the well-being it engenders and the aid which it gives to the expression of love.

I have explained all this because, though I have addressed myself in this book exclusively to women, I have, in fact, for the most part been putting over the man's point of view (an understanding of which is absolutely essential to your own approach to physical sex), and for this reason I did not want you to think that I do not appreciate the woman's view of the procreative aspect of sex.

May I repeat – for a man and a woman to develop their love to the full the physical experience of sex in which the woman obtains the greatest degree of physical satisfaction is as important to her as it is to her partner.

1. An Equal Partnership

Not many generations ago the Englishwoman was expected to play an entirely passive role in sexual relations. She was not credited with sexual feelings of her own. Her husband was the sexually active partner. When roused, he approached her and she allowed herself to be used as the instrument for the relief of his desires. Even if, at the same time, she achieved some sort of satisfaction herself, she gave no deliberate sign that she had, because to have given such a sign would have branded her as 'a not very nice woman'. In fact, there were quite large numbers of normally sexed women, needing only the minimum of preparation to achieve orgasm, who nevertheless went through the whole of their married lives without being aware not only that they were capable of orgasm but had as much right to achieve it as their husbands had to achieve theirs.

The peak of this strange state of affairs was reached at that period of the Victorian era when prudery in sexual matters came to such a pitch that quite often the legs of tables and grand pianos were covered with material, since they were thought to be indecent, and, if left uncovered, offensive to the female eye. Husbands and wives did not mention sex to one another even in the intimacy of their beds. Many married women went through their lives without even having seen the reproductive organs of their husbands, or of any other mature man. This applied equally to the husbands with regard to the female body, unless they had somewhat daring experiences with prostitutes.

It is easy to see that this attitude to the sexual parts of their bodies engendered in our ancestors a view of sex that made it something unclean, and for the woman, particularly, degrading. The 'nice' woman rejected sex for herself and participated in its practice only because her husband insisted upon it. Both she and her husband believed sexual intercourse to be the husband's prerogative. The husband expected, and demanded, that his wife should allow herself to be used as a means of giving him erotic pleasure; the wife accepted this role as merely one of the wifely responsibilities – and one of the more unpleasant ones – that marriage entailed.

To be fair, this attitude of the husband arose from his ignorance of his wife's sexual potentialities. As many men as women were unaware that a woman was capable of achieving orgasm. They had no notion that certain simple caresses could produce in their wives a sexual response which would heighten their own satisfaction at the same time that it made of their wives partners instead of mere instruments of gratification.

The attitude of the man towards the woman and his ignorance of the woman's capabilities were all part and parcel of a general ignorance not only of the woman's sexual functioning but of his own as well. Because he is capable of being aroused very easily and, once aroused, of achieving orgasm and relief very quickly, and because even the normally sexed woman takes anything from ten to fifteen minutes' application of a fairly skilful technique to achieve the state of arousal which he can achieve in seconds, either by a mental process of stimulation or by touch, the sexual act was confined purely to the insertion of the penis and the few movements necessary for him to achieve orgasm. Sexual intercourse was a brief encounter in which the husband received a few fleeting moments of pleasurable sensations and from which the wife achieved the knowledge that she had performed one of her wifely duties.

This made of intercourse not the warm and deeply intimate demonstration of mutual love, in which the giver received and the receiver gave, but a taking on the one part and nothing on the other. There can be little wonder, therefore, that women found the sexual act as repugnant as they were expected to find it, and that they felt themselves to be degraded by it.

Of course there must have been exceptions to this fairly general run of sexual behaviour. Highly passionate women, capable of achieving orgasm without much preparation, must certainly have existed then as they do now, and if they were married to sensitive and intelligent husbands they probably experienced a deep love as a result of this apparent miracle. It is nevertheless difficult for us, in our more enlightened generation, to understand exactly what the love-relationship of these ancestors of ours was.

Not long ago I was talking to a woman in her late eighties about this. 'I loved my husband, worshipped the ground he walked on', she said to me. 'He was a strong, passionate man, and until he died – he was sixty-two – he made frequent love to me, as you would say. Yes, I had some sensations, but only once or twice so strongly that they seemed to overwhelm me. I was a young girl then, and I was very frightened, and was always on guard that they should not happen. An acquantaince of mine, who had the reputation of being very fast, once asked me if I had ever had such experiences and didn't I think they were the most wonderful thing that could happen. I was horrified, and denied they had ever happened to me, and I told her that if she wished to remain on friendly terms with me she would never talk about such things to me again. I believe that nowadays women demand this kind of experience every time they are made love to. If they don't have it, don't they say they are unsatisfied women and dissatisfied wives and that they must divorce their husbands and find a man who can satisfy them in this way? Is this the modern definition of love? I gave my husband all he asked of me, and I was happy to do so. That was the extent of my love for him, and I would like to ask you whether you think love can be more extensive than that. I simply do not understand all this modern emphasis on sex.'

I had not the heart to say that I believed love could be and should be more extensive than that; nor to tell her that she had missed a great deal of what true sex communication can provide for both marriage partners; and I was, and am, equally perplexed by her generation's failure to discover the role of sex in marriage.

I have said 'her generation's failure'. As it happened, we have to thank one or two – a mere handful – of her generation for our present understanding of the role of sex in a relationship. They were enlightened men and women who, fortunately, were also blessed with a magnificent courage. It was due to men like Havelock Ellis and Charles Bradlaugh, and to women like Mrs Annie Besant, and, closer to our own times, Dr Marie Stopes, that ordinary men and women began to understand the sexual functions of the human male and female.

The movement for women's emancipation, following closely on the activities of the first pioneers of adult sex-education, gave a great impetus to the idea that women had sexual rights equal to those of men. Quite rightly it was argued that if a woman were capable of achieving the pleasure of orgasm, she ought to be granted its achievement as of right on equal terms with the man's demand that he should be allowed sexual satisfaction.

*   *   *

The First World War increased the impetus of women's emancipation, and then in 1918 Dr Marie Stopes began to publish her 'books on sexual hygiene', as she had to label them – *Married Love* in 1918, *Radiant Motherhood* in 1920, *Contraception* in 1921. Dr Stopes's first marriage was an unhappy one; her second was entirely satisfactory. It was a result of her early experiences which decided her to campaign for a wider understanding of the function of sex. With her second husband she opened a birth-control clinic in 1921, and in her books and articles used language which ordinary men and women could understand.

Her primary object was to improve the sexual status of women. Havelock Ellis, at the end of the last century and the beginning of this, had first put forward the then shocking theory that between husband and wife there was nothing impure about sex, and the perhaps even more amazing suggestion that there was nothing impure in sex at all. Dr Stopes took up this line, and with her unhesitating frankness she made her views known.

To achieve a satisfactory sex-life for women, while trying to teach them what their sexual functions were, she had to achieve the co-operation of the men. Among the men of her own generation she found her bitterest opponents, but among the younger men there were those who were prepared at least to try out her 'theory' that if they would be frank with their wives and really love them – as their marriage implied – they would help them to share in their own sexual pleasure. But this meant that the men had to learn a technique of practical sex behaviour, one of the dominant features of which was patience. As a reward for the exercise of such patience the wife would learn a technique also, and the two techniques combined would result in a much higher degree of pleasurable sensation than man had ever before dreamed himself capable of achieving.

Those who tried it found that she was right. She had only implied these rewards in her books. Her emphasis had been on establishing a sexual partnership which was on equal terms with the other partnership implied by marriage. At the same time, however, such a sexual partnership could not be achieved without the breakdown of the old ideas, taboos and views that existed between Victorian husbands and wives.

The discovery of sex – for that was what it was – proved exciting. The new relationship between husband and wife carried with it an onslaught on the old general view of the mystery of sex. If there was no mystery in sex for men and women who had taken the marriage vows, why need there be for those who had not? Besides, if the myth could be exploded for the young, how much better prepared they would be when they came to marry, and how much greater would be their chances of making a success of their marital sexual lives.

Sex education caught on, and inevitably frankness in sexual matters increased, until, with the added impetus of a second

world war – war is always a great inspirer of innovation – we
have reached today's position in which we find a hundred per
cent frankness between members of the same sex and between
husbands and wives; between parents and children almost
one hundred per cent; and a general and fast-moving tendency
towards one hundred per cent frankness between people of
both sexes, of all ages, who are quite unrelated to one another;
that is, an open and free approach by all.

*   *   *

I referred just now to 'a one hundred per cent frankness
between husbands and wives'. On second thoughts this is
probably an exaggeration. A truer assessment, I think, would
be a ninety-nine per cent frankness.

Why do I make this qualification?

The position today is this. In these statements I am referring
to the majority. There are still, of course, many men who are
ignorant of the sexual potentialities of women, or who, if they
are aware of them, are quite ignorant of the techniques of love-
making necessary to realize potentialities. Nevertheless, among
all classes there is a more extensive appreciation of the sexual
functions than there was forty, even twenty, years ago.

Men are aware that women are capable of orgasm; they
know that women take much longer to reach orgasm than they
do themselves; they know what they must do to help the
woman to reach orgasm; they are prepared to do it, and in
doing it to show great patience, for they know what rewards
will accrue to them both in the immediate intensification of
pleasure and, in the long term, in a more placid and happier
existence outside the sexual relationship.

Men know all this and more, and yet one influence of the
old way of thinking persists.

The man still looks upon himself as the natural instigator of
sexual activity. In every other respect, he admits, the woman
has a sexual life as necessary to her as his is to him; but in this
respect he does not expect her to make an approach to him
without waiting for him to make the first move.

Further than this, it does not occur to him that even if his partner should indicate that she desires to make love she could play the active role, while he submits to being the passive partner.

But something strange is happening here. I have discussed it with a fair number of my male acquaintances and almost without exception they have admitted that it had never occurred to them; then, after a moment or two's thought, some have said, 'It's funny, but now I come to think of it, I do sometimes imagine how nice it would be to be made love to; just to lie quietly and be stroked and caressed, and let things happen to me.'

There is this desire embedded in nearly all men, and certainly in all men of a passionate nature. It lies, for the most part, just under the surface of consciousness. Even when it comes to the surface, it remains there only for a moment or two before submerging again.

There is an explanation of it, of course. The sexually educated man has been taught two things which have been stressed as being of paramount importance to him as a lover: first, the measure of his success as a lover will be gauged by the degree of his ability to satisfy his partner – that is to say, not only help her to reach orgasm, but an orgasm which will be completely satisfying for her; and second, that his technique in achieving this will depend on his skill in controlling each stage of the intercourse – in other words, knowing what to do will be useless unless he can stimulate his partner to just the right degree of preparedness at the same time that he controls his own reactions. From which he argues that if his partner plays the active role it follows that she must be responsible for achieving her own orgasm; and if she is to make love to him, he may not be able, under the stimulus of her activities, to restrain his naturally quicker reactions to keep time with her naturally slower ones.

All this has no basis in fact. For all the average man's advance in knowledge of sexual functions and the practice of love techniques, it is still not widely known that the frequency of the woman's sexual urge can equal, and quite often exceed, that of the man.

Put another way, because the man is so easily aroused and

can so readily achieve orgasm, whereas the woman reacts much more slowly and requires comparatively prolonged stimulation to produce her orgasm, it is erroneously believed that the frequency of her urge is much less.

Again, there is a reason for this belief. A woman may feel the desire for intercourse, but unless she is stimulated the desire may subside. The woman may be conscious of this or not, but under the influence of the convention that she must await the initiative of the man she allows her desire to subside if he does not approach her.

This initial desire in the normally sexed woman is much less sharply defined and much less compulsive than the corresponding desire in the male. For her it is chiefly a sensation, though it is accompanied by a physical change in her sexual apparatus. This physical change, however, is invisible to her and it is not obtrusive.

This can certainly not be said of sexually aroused men. Besides the sensations of expectancy and urgency which surge in increasingly active and frequent waves in his loins, his erect penis, especially if the erection is a strong one, forces its attention upon him. If he is by himself it is extremely difficult for him to refrain from touching his penis, for by touching it he can temporarily relieve the throbbing tension, though the touching in fact can only provoke increased stimulation of desire in the long run.

It is true that if a man makes a conscious effort, and is strong-willed enough to divert his thoughts so that he ceases to be acutely aware of the sensations in his loins and penis, the erection will in time subside and the desire disappear. But this is only a temporary retreat on the part of the desire. Though hours may intervene, and even though by this time he may be asleep, the desire and the erection will return, and only orgasm can effectively quell them. Again there is a physical explanation, but I will go into the details of it later.

The underlying idea of re-educating men and women in the practice of sex was, as I have said, to raise the sexual status of the woman and at the same time achieve several other improvements which affected the man as much as her. When it had been established that a woman had an equal right to orgasm and satisfaction, she became a partner of the man in their sexual activity. Acting, I suppose, on the principle that reforms must not be rushed if permanent changes are to be effected, and since, because of his naturally more agressive sexuality, they had selected the man as their main agent, the pioneer sex-educators laid stress upon his role in the sexual act. Their wisdom in doing so was impeccable, but those who have followed those early innovators – and there have been many scores of them – have continued to place the same degree of emphasis on the man's responsibilities.

It is true that, little by little, the woman's role has been increased. She has been told, for example, that it is possible for her to complement the technique of her partner in his arousal of her by certain activities of her own, and that there are caresses which she can employ which will heighten her partner's sensations and thus increase his satisfaction. But, though by implication it has been suggested that she is a partner in love-making, it is nevertheless also implied that she is a junior partner; and this I do not believe to be right.

*　　　*　　　*

It is agreed that a woman has as much right as a man to the fullest satisfaction it is possible to achieve from the sex-act; that the fulfilment of the demands her sexuality makes on her is as important to her as her partner's is to him; that together they can lay down a basis of mutual physical harmony which can bestow incalculable benefits on their partnership as a whole. This being so, to my way of thinking, the status of the woman in the sexual relationship is *equal* partnership – the status which incidentally confers on her in every way a happy and satisfactory marriage.

Equal partnership, once admitted, presupposes the additional right of the woman to take the sexual initiative whenever she feels like it. Once this is accepted by the man and from my contact with many married men I honestly believe that there will be very few, if any, who will permanently reject it, though there may be initial, half-hearted attempts to do so – the sexual life of both will become richer and even more satisfactory and satisfying. There will come into being a new conception of the sexual partnership, because now it is a true sharing in which both partners have equal responsibilities.

It is no brilliantly original idea that I am advocating. It may be a new idea to many Englishmen and women, but among other peoples it has been the common practice for much longer than memory.

*   *   *

Among most oriental peoples the girl is prepared for marriage much more carefully than the man, and a large part of her preparation is devoted to learning from older and experienced women the technique of making love. She is taught that it is part of wifely duty to satisfy her husband sexually; and not merely to satisfy his urge but to make it possible for him to experience the most pleasurable erotic sensations that technique is capable of producing.

This is the opposite of our own conception of the male and female roles, so what about a woman's own needs? The oriental woman is wise and cunning – though no wiser nor more cunning than her western sister – and she is as deeply aware of the pleasure to be gained for herself from satisfactory love-making as any other woman is. Her technique, therefore, provides that she shall be able to achieve this pleasure by her own efforts and in co-operating with her husband.

In oriental marriages the woman, at the outset, is the more experienced, or at least the more sexually knowledgeable partner, though the man has not been entirely forgotten. He has been told, and experience is not long in confirming the truth of it, that the greatest contribution he can make to intercourse is the control of his climax; and that next in importance is his virility – that is, his ability to obtain and to retain for some time a powerful erection. Having made sure that he possesses the second – and if it does not arise naturally there are many potions to which he can resort which will promote the condition – and having acquired a fair degree of the first, he is taught a few very simple caresses.

It is he who makes the first approaches. But it is a polite

fiction in which the couple are indulging, necessary to the husband's self-respect; for the eastern husband believes himself to be the master of his household, the dominant partner of his marriage and his marriage-bed.

But the husband having made the initial approach, and meeting the other conditions required of him, it is not long before the wife takes over the conduct of the intercourse. She does it unobtrusively, and if challenged would deprecate any praise of her art. From the very first act of love she demonstrates to her partner the sweet pleasure that can come from skilful love-making. Within a short time of marriage the husband realizes that there are other skills which he can contribute. There is a period of experimentation during which the heights of erotic sensations are sought, and because, during this period, a complete frankness inevitably develops between husband and wife the sexual relationship of the couple becomes an equal partnership in which the technique of both is deemed an essential contribution.

Nor is civilization a necessary prerequisite for this kind of sexual behaviour. Many peoples in Africa, in Asia and in the islands of the Pacific educate their women from an early age to become adepts in the art of making love. They may not be able to read, nor drive a motor-car, nor understand electricity; but they do appreciate that the more pleasurable the sensations or orgasmic climax are, the more satisfying the other aspects of the marriage relationship will be.

I do not know sufficient of the history of French and Italian sex-practices to be able to say for how long the French woman and the Italian woman have been enjoying the role of equal sex partnership, but I do know that what I am suggesting for the English woman has been common usage in France and Italy for at least seventy years. France and Italy are not the only two European countries in which the woman is expected to undertake an active role in love-making. I have mentioned them specifically because they are best known to me personally, and, I imagine, to my readers.

Many of us have been aware for a long time that the French have a very different approach to sex from our own, even if we have not known in what respects it differs. We have had a vague idea that they permit much greater licence that we do. We have a picture of a Frenchman who does not hesitate to make sexual advances to any woman who attracts him; of a Frenchman who treats love-making as an art-cum-science. And if such a Frenchman does exist, naturally the French-woman also exists who makes it possible for him to do these things.

There is a tiny grain of truth in this, but the real truth is that in the sexual history of France there was never a period of Victorian prudery. Sex for the Frenchman has always been an integral part of living, and a source of much pleasure. He discovered long ago that if he admitted his wife to equal partnership in the sexual relationship the enjoyment of the exquisite and unique physical experience of love-making could be greatly enhanced. He found, too, that by admitting his wife to this status he was not undermining his own status as the dominant partner in the marriage relationship as a whole, nor his leadership in its sexual aspects. So the Frenchman encouraged his wife to make herself adept at love-making.

So, if I am proposing no original approach to sex, I am also not proposing anything which an Englishwoman could not accept on grounds of indelicacy as defined by the standards of western civilization, or of temperament; for with regard to the latter, the technique involved must, if it is to be successful, match the temperament.

Let me repeat what I am proposing.

The woman, I say, should not be the permanently passive partner in a sexual relationship. If at any time she feels she would like to indulge in intercourse and her partner gives no sign of making any approach to her, she should not hesitate to take the initiative herself. In this way, she can procure for herself what she does not yet possess in the sexual aspect of her marriage – equal partnership.

She will demonstrate that she is as much a person in her own right sexually as she is, say, as housewife or career woman. In achieving this status both she and her partner will acquire a new appreciation of one another. As a result of this they will enjoy an intimacy of far greater depth than any they have previously enjoyed; and this, in turn, cannot fail to contribute to the greater success of the partnership as a whole. Anything which tends to bring about the latter can only be good.

*   *   *

So, in the following pages I am going to discuss sex chiefly from the woman's point of view. Of course, I shall explain the man's approach to sex, how he functions sexually and how he performs sexually; but the main emphasis will be on how his approach, his functioning and his performance affect the woman. By the time I have finished I hope I shall have succeeded in opening up new vistas not only with regard to your sexual life but with regard to your life as a whole.

But before I go on may I make one or two things quite clear?

I am going to assume that you know precisely how a baby is conceived, and what happens at ovulation, menstruation, during pregnancy and birth. For this reason I shall not discuss the processes of conception, pregnancy and birth, and I shall refer to these processes only in their relationship to love-making for pleasure.

I am also going to assume that you and your partner are physically normally constructed people. I shall not, therefore, deal with such questions as sterility and fertility, impotence and frigidity.

Then I am going to assume that you are living with your partner because you love him, and that one of the reasons why you submit to having intercourse with him is that while you are joined together and afterwards, while you are still in his arms and he in yours, before you go to sleep or return to the more ordinary things of the world, you experience a deep affection for him which brings you great happiness, and which for you both translates intercourse into a visible expression of your love. You may know that you love your partner, you may *tell* him that you do, may try to show him in a hundred ways, big or little, that you do, and he may try to assure you of his love for you in the same way; but nothing that you or he can say or do, and most certainly the latter, can demonstrate – so that you can feel it and so know that it is happening without doubt – the 'one-person' that a man and woman in love should try to be as undeniably as the actual penetration of the penis deep into the most secret places of the woman's body.

If you are really in love, you must have realized this; and since you must also have realized that the greater degree of physical ecstasy you experience at the moment of climax, the greater is your feeling of tenderness, affection and love for your man, then you will understand how very important it is that both of you should know how to make love in a way that will make the physical experience such that other physical experiences cannot come anywhere near it, either in the actual sensations or in the mental attitude which is the natural and inevitable result of the physical satisfaction achieved. The very phrase 'to make love' – which, in my view, has so much greater meaning than the scientific descriptions such as 'sexual intercourse', 'copulation', 'coitus', or even the lay 'sex-act' – describes what you should be doing when you and your partner participate in intercourse, and I suggest that you should keep it always in mind.

I am also going to assume that you have decided for yourselves your religious and moral attitudes towards sex. If you are not a religious person this side will present no difficulties, and certainly neither religious convictions nor the lack of them will affect the quality of your love for your partner, or your approach to love-making. If, on the other hand, you are a religious woman there are one or two things to which, though I am certain they will have occurred to you, I feel I must draw attention.

The greater part of the enjoyment of living comes from the pleasure provided by the sensations which the various parts of the body produce. For example, the pleasure of eating and drinking comes from the taste-buds, the pleasure of music by way of the ears, of art by way of the eyes. Such pleasures as these we accept as natural corollaries of our body's functions, and regard the enjoyment of them as a right.

But as God created the organs by which you taste, see and hear, so He created the parts of your body with which you make love; and as He did so, He implanted in them the means of deriving a physical and mental pleasure quite different from the pleasure derived from other parts of the body, both in the nature and in the intensity of the sensations. Having taken the trouble to do this, He obviously intended that these parts of the body should be used, and used in such a way that the greatest degree of this particular pleasure should be achieved. There can be no questioning, therefore, of sexual activity between husband and wife, and, it follows, no justification for feelings of guilt. In fact, if there is any sin attaching to the sexual activity of man and woman, it exists only in the feelings of guilt – the feelings of guilt are the sin. I shall be referring again to this question of guilt and sin when I shall try to define 'normal' sexual activity between man and woman.

What I have said in these last two paragraphs I regard as of paramount importance, and at the risk of being a bore I am going to repeat them.

You were given the sexual parts of your body to use; these parts of your body are endowed with qualities capable of providing fantastically pleasurable physical sensations which in turn produce mental stimuli as well as mental peace; as you take it for granted that you are expected to develop your talents of mind and body in other directions, so you need have no hesitation on religious and moral grounds in using sex to add to the enrichment of life; in the final analysis, sexual activity is a function as natural as eating, sleeping, listening to music, reading or cooking.

It is this basis – love of the partners for one another and the naturalness of sex activity as a bodily function – that I intend to set out what man and woman should achieve from love-making and how they should make love.

But before I go on to this may I stress just once more – because it is such an important point – that sexual relations are not composed of the physical aspects alone. The emotions are deeply involved, and it is just as necessary that these should be satisfied as that the physical sexual demands of both partners should be.

As I have said earlier, what I am going to talk about in the following pages is almost exclusively the physical side of sex. This is not because I believe this to be the *most* important aspect of sex, but because it is widely agreed by the experts in these matters that where the physical performance of sex is satisfactory it generally follows that the emotional responses of the partners are satisfactory also. On the other hand, no matter how emotionally responsive the partners may be at the beginning – in other words, no matter how much in love they may be – if love-making does not produce physical satisfaction, sooner or later, in the majority of cases, the emotional side is going to be affected. When this happens, it is then that the partnership begins to tremble on its foundations.

Having said this, I must ask you not to misunderstand me. Human marital relations are a very complicated affair, and I am not saying that if you make love in such a way that the satisfaction of your physical desires is one hundred per cent this will automatically make your partnership a happy and successful one.

What I am saying is that if you do make love in such a way that the physical demands of your sex are satisfied, you are going to have a far easier task in making a success of things as a whole than if your sexual desires remain unsatisfied.

So long as you realize that, though I am dealing in this book with purely physical matters, I am very alive to the emotional aspects of the sexual relationship, I do not think I need excuse myself for having concentrated on physical sex. Emotions, especially those generated by love, are very individual things, and I do not think anyone can be told how they should respond emotionally, except in very very general terms. It is possible, however, to describe the techniques of making love which can lead to physical satisfaction if adapted to personal use, and since, as I have said, physical satisfaction prepares the way for emotional response, no harm can be done in trying to help people towards the attainment of physical satisfaction.

Lastly, I should not like you to think that if you follow religiously what I have set out here all your problems will automatically be solved. This book is a guide. In it I throw out ideas – which quite a number of people have found helpful – but it is up to you to select from them such as you think, and may find by trying them out, will assist you in developing and maturing your love for your partner and his for you.

2. The Anatomy of Love-Making

In order to know what to do, no matter whether it is baking a cake, making a dress, playing the piano, or painting a picture, it is necessary to have some idea of what the things you have to work with are capable. Admittedly, there are many things we can do, and do well, without knowing exactly how we do them. Have you ever stopped to think, for example, how your food is digested? You eat and leave your body to do the rest-- though sometimes, if you did understand the digestive processes, you might take more care over what you put into your stomach. It is, of course, quite possible to make love without understanding what happens in your body while you are doing it. On the other hand, if you do understand what happens, you will almost certainly be able to do it better.

Let us assume that you are listening to a performance of Beethoven's *Emperor Concerto*. You may know nothing about music and yet receive quite a lot of pleasure from this performance; but supposing you knew that when Beethoven was composing the first movement he worked to a strict set of rules – that the first section of this movement introduced a theme and the second section a second theme and that subsequent sections developed these two themes, and finally the first theme would bring the movement to a triumphant conclusion?

If you knew this you would be able to recognize the themes, watch for their statement and appreciate the skill with which the composer developed them. Each time a part of each theme came into the music you would recognize it; or, knowing by the rules that this must happen, you would wait with excitement to see how the composer was going to handle it. Because of this would be much closer to the music and to the performers, and more appreciative of the conductor's interpretation; consequently your pleasure would be much greater than when you listened without realizing what was happening except that beautiful sounds were being made.

This is very true of love-making. As I said a moment ago, it is possible to take part in sexual intercourse and derive some pleasure from it merely by knowing that the man places his erect penis inside you and moves it backwards and forwards until a small amount of fluid is expelled from him into you. It is not necessary to know that the male member is called the penis, that part of you which receives it is called the vagina and that the fluid expelled is called semen, in order to complete a fairly successful intercourse; but neither of you is really and truly making love. You are merely allowing yourself to be the means of providing your partner and yourself with certain sensations.

If, on the other hand, you know why the movements of the penis within you eventually cause the man to expel the semen into you, you will also know that certain sensitive nerves in the tip of the penis are acted upon by the gentle friction of the special texture of the walls of your vagina in such a way that muscles within his body are encouraged to contract, and that the contractions press upon the vessels which hold the semen and force it along a series of tubes until it leaves him and comes into you, at the same time providing him with extremely pleasurable sensations. These sensations, you will be aware, are one of the reasons for your partner wanting to make love to you; and you will also undoubtedly know now that if he does this or that he will obtain these sensations sooner or later, and thus you will understand why he sometimes behaves as he does.

✻   ✻   ✻

It is probably more true of the sexual organs than of any other part of the body that a knowledge of how they work is essential to make them perform with the highest degree of efficiency. In fact, I am inclined to delete the word *probably* from this sentence and say bluntly and sweepingly – 'Your sexual organs cannot give their best performance until you know how they work.

This is not to say that every time you make love you must consciously tell yourself that at any given moment such and such is happening, has happened or will happen because this or that part of you or your partner is doing such and such. Once you have learned to ride a bicycle proficiently, each time you mount it you do not have to concentrate on keeping your balance; this has become second nature to you, and as you pedal along you can devote your consciousness to the enjoyment of what is going on around you. Similarly, once you have learned what happens when you are making love, with a little experience you can take part without concentrating on the mechanics of it. You will perform the mechanics, but the actual mechanical side will be second nature to you, and your mind will be left free to concentrate on the achievement of the greatest possible pleasure.

I do not want to seem to be pressing this point unduly, but it is really of extreme importance. All, or nearly all, of the hundreds of organs which constitute our bodies require help and encouragement from us. Muscles will atrophy if not exercised and will perform better and last longer if looked after with care. As you grow older you will puff and pant as you go upstairs unless you have taken care to exercise your lungs and have not strained your heart when younger.

The sex organs need a similar encouragement and assistance, but with this difference: they need help, not to function well, but in order to function at their best. Unlike most of the other limbs, they require this assistance each time they are asked to function. Apart from their primary task of reproduction – and this role I am not concerned with in this book – their function is to provide the greatest degree of erotic pleasure of which they are capable. Left to themselves they can carry out their reproductive role only, though this is accompanied by a certain degree of erotic pleasure. But when they are called into play in their role as instruments of love-making they are required to produce the most intense sensations of which they are capable, since it is the intensity of these sensations which provides the deepest feelings of physical satisfaction, for from these feelings flow the mental satisfaction, the affection and the love which enrich the partnership. In other words, the sex organs are not exercised to assure the continuance of their functioning; they are brought into play as a *means* of binding man and woman together more firmly and more explicitly in their relationship.

Before we can consider their functions we must consider the organs themselves. I am sure that what I am going to write in the remainder of this chapter you will know already. I must recapitulate, however, in order that the explanations I shall give later may be more easily understood by this information being fresh in your mind.

The Female Sex Organs

It is customary to say that the woman's sex organs are internal, carried inside the body. Compared with the man's, and from the point of view that none of them is readily visible, this is true. On the other hand, certain of them are situated outside the body, and can be seen if looked for. These external organs are, for the purpose of satisfactory love-making, among the most important of the female's sexual apparatus.

The first of these exterior organs are the folds of flesh which cover and protect the entrance to the vagina, which for our purpose is the most important *internal* organ.

There are two sets of these folds, and they are referred to as the large or outer lips and the small or inner lips. The large lips are covered with ordinary skin and hair, and enclose two other organs, which I shall mention presently, as well as the small lips and the entrance to the vagina.

If the outer lips are pressed apart by the fingers, they are seen to cover another, smaller fold of flesh. This fold is the small or inner lips, and it will be noted that the skin covering them is smooth, pink and different in texture, and particularly in sensitivity, from any other skin of our bodies.

Embedded in this skin, and covered by the inner lips, are the two other organs to which I have already referred. They are situated one above the other; the upper one, known as the clitoris, in the apex of the fold formed by the inner lips.

The clitoris – the most important of the external organs – consists of two parts. There is a bulbous head about the size of a pea appearing above the surface of the flesh in which it is embedded, and a short, proportionately slim shaft of specially composed flesh running into and eventually rooted in the flesh, to which the head is attached.

About an inch or a little below the clitoris is the second organ which has no sexual significance whatsoever. It is the opening of the urethra, the tube by which the bladder is emptied of urine.

Still further below the urethral opening is the entrance to the vagina, which is covered by the same special kind of skin as the covering of the inner lips and the flesh they protect.

The vagina is a sheath which goes up into the body. It is usually between three and a half and four inches long, but it has elastic qualities which allow it to stretch both sideways and lengthways so that it may accommodate any size of penis.

The walls of the vagina consist of very delicate membranes, which are soft to the touch and have such qualities that they react on the very sensitive nerves near the tip of the penis when the latter is moved against them, and they are responsible for promoting the muscular spasms in the man which bring about the expulsion of the semen.

The womb, in which the fertilized egg develops into a baby, is a hard, almost bone-like hollow structure. In the unpregnant woman it, too, is about three inches in length, but it possesses expansive qualities even more extraordinary than the vagina, which allow it to swell to many, many times its quiescent size as the developing baby grows. It is shaped like an inverted pear, and the tapered end fits into the top end of the vagina. In the tapered end is the entrance through which the male sperms swim to meet the egg. This tapered end is known as the cervix, or neck, of the womb, and while the womb has no significance for us the cervix has, as will be seen later.

The other female sex organs – with which we are also

unconcerned, since they play no part in love-making – are two sets of ovaries, which hold the eggs; the follicles, which surround the eggs and burst when the egg is ripe, thus releasing it; the Fallopian tubes in which the mature egg waits to be fertilized by the male sperm, and down which it moves into the womb, either when it has been fertilized or after it has ceased to be capable of fertilization to make way for the next mature egg.

The clitoris, the outer and inner lips, the vagina, the womb, the ovaries and the Fallopian tubes are known as the primary female sex organs. But you have also secondary sex organs – the breasts.

I can never quite decide whether the breasts are considered secondary sex organs because they are placed at some distance from and have no direct connection with the primary organs; or whether indeed they are considered sex organs at all because they play a role in the feeding of the baby after birth and are physically affected by pregnancy.

But whatever may be the explanation, they have a definite significance for us, because they are connected in a very intricate way with the nervous system of the primary sex organs and play a very definite role in the sexual arousal of the woman.

When the woman is sexually aroused, her nipples, like the male penis, become engorged with blood, and stand out stiff and erect. If, in that state, they are gently fondled by the fingers or the lips, they send down sensations to the primary sex organs which stimulate the latter to a higher state of arousal. In some women, caressing the nipples can have such an intensive effect on the primary sex organs that orgasm can be reached purely by this means, without the penetration of the penis or the stimulation of any of the primary sex organs.

To sum up, the female organs with which love-making is concerned are the clitoris, the outer and inner lips, the actual entrance to the vagina, the cervix and the breasts.

You will notice that I have not included the vagina iself; and my reasons for not doing so are these: the clitoris, the lips, the vaginal entrance, the cervix and the breasts are organs richly endowed with those nerves which, when stimulated, produce orgasm. Though the vaginal walls are also rich in nerves, curiously they do not seem to be so susceptible to stimulation-to-orgasm as are the nerves of the other organs mentioned. Some medical men maintain that they are, because logically it would seem that they ought to be; and also because it is they which stimulate the penis to orgasm. Any male can achieve orgasm by simply moving his penis within the vagina. On the other hand, he can as readily reach orgasm by the stimulation of the penile nerves with the fingers, by rubbing gently against a smooth surface, or by the oral contact of the partner.

I do not want to become involved here in a medical argument on this point. All I can say is that there are statistics which show that a very large number of women seem to achieve their greatest sexual arousal from stimulation of the clitoris rather than from stimulation of the vaginal walls. But in any event, even if the vaginal walls are sensitive, it takes a much longer time for the woman so equipped to achieve orgasm in this way than if she is subjected to clitoris stimulation. I even go so far as to urge man and woman to resort deliberately to clitoris stimulation even if she can achieve orgasm by means of vaginal stimulation alone.

A little later I shall be referring again to the sensitive qualities of the vagina to the friction set up by the man's penis. For the time being, I would like to leave it at what I have just said.

So much, then, for the female organs.

The Male Sex Organs

The male organs also lie partly inside the body and partly outside. The whole male system is somewhat less intricate than the female, and there are only two organs which have any significance for us – the penis and the scrotum containing the testicles – both of which are visible.

The scrotum lies at the back of and extends somewhat below the relaxed penis, and is suspended entirely below the erect penis. It is a pouch of ordinary skin which contains the two testicles.

Each testicle consists of about half-a-mile of tiny hollow tubing and is in fact a sperm-producing factory. The testicles are connected by other tubes to two small vessels situated inside the man's belly, one on either side of the base of the bladder. These vessels are known as the seminal vesicles, and they produce a fluid which eventually leaves the penis as a constituent of the semen. The two tubes join together at the base of the seminal vesicles and pass into a gland called the prostate, from which they emerge to join the urethral tube which runs from the bladder through the penis and thus serves the double purpose of expelling the urine and the semen.

As soon as the penis becomes erect a small muscle, known as the sphincter, which is situated at the exit to the bladder, clamps itself tightly round the urethral tube and closes the bladder so that urine cannot be expelled or escape during sexual arousal and intercourse.

The prostate gland produces a fluid called seminal fluid. The difference between what is meant by *seminal fluid* and *semen* should be understood. The fluid which is ejaculated during orgasm – it is a pale, milky-coloured, fluid, thick, viscous substance – is *semen*, and it is made up of seminal fluid, the fluid produced by the seminal vesicles, and sperms. If you saw specimens of seminal fluid and semen you would not be able to tell the difference between them unless you observed them under a microscope, for though the teaspoonful of semen which the man discharges with each ejaculation contain the amazing number of between 250,000,000 and 400,000,000 sperms, the sperm is so small that even in such vast quantities it cannot be seen with the naked eye. The manufacture of sperm by the testicles is a never-ceasing process. How many billions of sperms the testicles are capable of holding has not yet been calculated; but when the figures I have just quoted as being expelled with each ejaculation are considered, the number must be really astronomical.

The sperm itself is a small, rather tadpole-like organism, consisting of a head to which a powerful tail is attached. While it is in the testicles and in the tubes it is inert and quite incapable of movement by itself. The moment, however, that it joins the seminal fluid it becomes wildly active. It lashes its tail powerfully and by doing so swims about rapidly in the seminal fluid. The impetus which it obtains while doing this enables it to leave the seminal fluid, which is deposited near the entrance to the womb, and to swim through the cervix, right through the womb and up into the Fallopian tubes to the woman's egg.

This is an extraordinary long journey for such a small being, and since sperms, like any other creatures, are not all equally strong, many give up on the way and never reach their objective. A good analogy is the mating of bees. There is only one queen-bee in each swarm of bees, but there are several hundreds of males. When the queen-bee is ready for mating, she flies off and is followed by every male in the swarm. A large number of males are unable to keep up with her, and of those who can it is the strongest one, able to fly the fastest and catch her up, who eventually mates with her and fertilizes her.

Exactly the same thing happens with egg and sperm. By the time the Fallopian tubes are reached – the journey from the cervix to the tubes represents to the sperms a distance of a hundred or so man miles – the sperms have thinned out considerably. Probably only a hundred or so out of the initial millions ever reach the entrance to the tubes themselves; and it is the strongest *one* that reaches the egg first, that at last joins with it and fertilizes it.

An understanding of the prodigious journey undertaken by the sperm, and the hazards which lie in wait along the way, will make it possible to appreciate why the testicles are required to manufacture such fantastic numbers of sperms. Nevertheless, this example of nature's generosity must always surprise and bewilder.

When the man is not sexually aroused, and particularly so when he is warm, the scrotum hangs slack and loose. When he is aroused, however, it contracts. The same thing happens when he is cold, even though he is not roused. In its loose state the skin of the scrotum is scarcely sensitive to touch at all; contracted, however, it does become quite sensitive to very light caresses, and though the degree of sensitivity of the scrotum is very low compared with the sensitivity of the whole of the erect penis, and particularly the special nerves, to which I shall presently refer, the right degree of caress can add much to the intensity of the state of arousal. The greatest care must be taken that only very light touches are made, for the testicles are very tender and the smallest excess of pressure can be sufficiently painful to destroy all erotic sensations. So while the scrotum is a source of erotic sensation, unless its qualities and reactions are understood the whole object of giving it attention during love-making can be completely nullified.

The penis is the most important male organ in love-making. It is a tubular construction consisting of three sections of sponge-like tissue, through the middle of which run the urethra-sperm duct, a number of arteries and a small number of small blood vessels. It terminates in an almost cone-shaped head, known as the glans penis. On the upper side, where the glans joins the body of the penis, there is a slightly prominent ridge.

The glans is covered with a loose fold of ordinary skin, called the foreskin, which can be pulled right back under the ridge, thus exposing the whole of the glans.

The foreskin can be removed completely by a simple surgical operation known as circumcision. Among the Jews and Muslims circumcision is a religious rite. All male Jews are circumcised when they are eight days old in a religious ceremony. Among non-Jews circumcision is not practised as a rite or obligation, but this is not to say that the operation is not performed at all.

It is essential, for various reasons, that the foreskin should be capable of being pulled over the glans, but sometimes the opening at the end is too small to allow this to be done, or the baby's mother has failed to stretch the opening in the days immediately following birth. In such cases the doctor will invariably advise circumcision.

In recent years, however, even where the foreskin can be retracted naturally, circumcision has become quite fashionable, chiefly for reasons of hygiene. Small particles of grit and dust can collect between the foreskin and the sensitive head of the penis, and if the boy or man does not take care to wash the penis at the very least once daily, these particles can set up an irritation. This irritation causes erection, even when the man is not conscious of any other sexual stimulation; and the erection can last either until the irritants are removed or orgasm has been brought about. With their well-known aversion to soap and water, boys are more inclined to resort to the latter by means of masturbation, and this method of relief, which is only temporary, since the removal of the irritants is the sole cure, is thought by many parents to encourage an undue, and unnecessary, interest in sex.

Also, in the uncircumcized man, secretions of mucous which from time to time are exuded by the penis collect under the ridge of the base of the glans, between the ridge and the foreskin, and form a solid deposit, known as smegma. Smegma not only gives off an offensive odour, but it, too, causes irritation, unless the penis is carefully washed at least daily. In the circumcized penis smegma cannot form.

But there is another reason in favour of circumcision. The head of the penis is its most sensitive part. On its underside, where the foreskin is attached right to the tip of the glans, is a mass of extremely sensitive nerves. The slightest touch of these is sufficient to induce erection, and continued stimulation, often less than two minutes in duration, can produce orgasm. They are, in fact, the orgasm-producing nerves. (The ridge is also highly sensitive to stimulation.)

If these nerves are unprotected by the foreskin, in time they lose some of their sensitivity. They are so powerful, however, that *they retain their orgasm-producing qualities throughout the man's life.* But the advantage of a partial loss of sensitivity is that they need longer stimulation to produce orgasm and so lessen the gap between the time the man requires to reach orgasm and the time required by the woman, besides making it a good deal easier for the man to control the rhythm of his progress to orgasm.

It would appear that there are quite a number of women who are not at all clear about the physical appearance which circumcision gives to the penis. I once heard of a case of a young wife who sought expert advice only a few months after her marriage. She was the only girl in a family of four, and the parents had had progressive ideas about the sex-education of their children. They themselves had had no inhibitions about letting the children see them naked, and from birth until they were adults the children had been accustomed to seeing one another naked.

None of the brothers had been circumcized, but the young woman's husband had been. She had heard of circumcision, but did not know precisely what it entailed. It appeared that the husband was highly passionate, and, despite the fact that he had been circumcized, in the first few weeks of marriage he had had the quite common experience of young husbands of what is known as premature ejaculation. (By premature ejaculation is meant that the man achieves orgasm and expels his semen either before or immediately upon inserting his penis into the vagina, which makes it very difficult, and often impossible, for him to continue love-making until his partner has reached her orgasm.)

The husband was apparently very distressed by what he regarded as his failure to satisfy his wife, and his wife felt extremely sorry for him. She realized that the appearance of his penis was not like that of her brothers, but did not know that this was due to circumcision. She wondered, in fact, if it were some kind of deformity which might be responsible, in part, if not wholly, for her husband's premature ejaculation.

Though they were completely frank with one another about sex, she hesitated to put her doubts to her husband, for fear that she would add worry to his distress. Fortunately, she had the courage and intelligence to seek expert advice herself – and was assured that her husband suffered from no deformity, but had merely been circumcized.

'Oh, that's what it is!' she exclaimed. 'I know that circumcision means cutting the foreskin, but I didn't realize it meant removing it altogether.'

She was also told that her husband's tendency to premature ejaculation was fairly common among young and very ardent lovers and that it could be eliminated by experience and technique. She was urged to persuade her husband to seek expert advice himself which he did, and the matter was very quickly put right.

When the man is not sexually roused, the penis is soft and hangs limply downwards over the scrotum. You will recall that it is composed of what I described as a sponge-like substance.

When the man begins to experience sexual desire, the thousands of little cavities in this substance are filled with blood. This has the effect of causing the penis to swell considerably, to become very hard and to stand up stiffly and vertically in the direction of the lower part of the stomach. In this condition, the man is said to have an erection. If the erection is a strong one, the penis often touches the stomach, even when the man is standing up. Erection is essential before the penis can be inserted in the vagina.

It is necessary to understand that the strength of the erection is not always the same. If your partner is tired, his penis may stiffen only sufficiently to lift it to a horizontal position. It is stiff enough to enter the vagina, however, and normally once it has been inserted it becomes fully erect, no matter how tired he may be.

Erection is essential for the achievement of orgasm, but the latter can be reached even when the erection is not a full one.

In every man the basic form of the penis is the same, but like other organs of his body, it can differ in size from individual to individual. This is one of the reasons why the vagina has been endowed with its elastic qualities.

The size of the penis has no relation to the man's general physical build. A large, broad-shouldered Adonis can possess a small penis; a small, thin man a large penis. The average-sized penis, however, when relaxed is between three and a half to four inches long and three to three and a half inches in circumference. In full erection, the average erect penis is about six inches long and four and a half inches in circumference. The large penis seldom exceeds eight to nine inches in length, with a corresponding circumference, but such examples are extremely rare. In general there are many penises smaller than average.

Now, it cannot be stressed sufficiently that the size of the penis has absolutely no effect whatsoever on the achievement of conception, nor, what is much more important in our consideration, on the intensity of orgasm, in its capacity to provide the woman with the greatest degree of orgasmic enjoyment and satisfaction.

In fact, there have been (and are) cases in which a much-above-average penis has caused the woman discomfort and either made it very difficult for her to achieve orgasm at all or, at best, given her only mild satisfaction. The reason for this will become clear when we begin to consider the actual technique of love-making.

Before I go on to talk about other male sexual characteristics, I want to say a word or two about the relationship of the penis, its size and erectile performance, to the man's psychological representation of himself to himself.

Whether the man is conscious of it or not, his penis has for him a significance above and beyond its merely physical role as the organ by which he begets children, or by which he can experience the most exquisite of all physical sensations, or through which, in intercourse, he can visibly assure his partner of the emotional bond of deep affection (love) which he feels for her. The man has always regarded himself as the superior sex but in order to reassure himself he finds he is in need of a symbol which will visibly demonstrate his manhood.

It is natural, we must admit, that he should select as this symbol that organ whose functions are entirely devoted to the expression of his male sexuality. This has been so ever since man began. The male penis, not the female womb or vagina, has been, and still is, propitiated by primitive man as the source of fertility.

But as he regards his penis as the symbol of his manhood, so he is jealous of its looks and performance. Though most normal men consciously appear satisfied with the size of their penis, in a great many, if not all, men there is a hidden wish that it were larger. This wish becomes a conscious thought in quite a number of men with a penis of the dimensions I have given as average, but it is particularly so in the cases of men with a below-average-size member. Such men are extremely sensitive about the size of their penis and any remarks about it, even made entirely in fun, are taken very much to heart.

Stekel, a famous pioneer sexual psychologist, has recorded a case of a young man who went with a prostitute. In the course of their preparatory caresses the woman teased the young man about the smallness of his penis. He was so hurt by her gibes that he immediately lost his erection, and until his treatment and cure by Stekel was never again able to achieve an erection while in bed with a woman.

This is, of course, a somewhat extreme case, but it does nevertheless happen that the feelings of inadequacy as a lover which a small penis may engender in its possessor can be transferred to practically every aspect of a man's life. Such men usually do not know that a small penis is just as capable of providing the partner with complete sexual satisfaction as a large one; and are ignorant of the compensating technique which will remove all possibility of failure to be an adequate lover. Where the man has realized these points, and has set himself to acquire and perfect a compensating technique, he is more often than not a much more satisfactory lover than a man more generously equipped, but who relies too much on his penis for his success as a sexual partner.

I have dwelt on this point because it is one not usually talked about by men, even among themselves. The teasing by men-friends, or their direct references to a man's penile smallness, can have an effect as upsetting as such teasing or references by a woman. So men, respecting their fellow-men's feelings on the subject, take care to avoid the risk of damaging a fellow-man's self-respect. Certainly no man will draw the attention of his woman partner to his so-called deficiency, and for this reason she is quite unlikely to have any knowledge of this specific male problem.

But it is obvious that it is most important she should be aware of it; and not only must she be aware of it, she must be constantly on her guard, for it is quite possible for her unwittingly to do the damage she would most anxiously avoid. After the penetration of the penis, as the climax of the orgasm approaches with gathering impetus, the woman often experiences the sensation of wanting the penis to thrust more deeply into her, though it is already as deep as its length will allow – a fact of which the man is very well aware – even though the penis may be of average or above-average length, and despite the fact that the sensations provided by the far end of the vagina are not intense, if they exist at all, and contribute nothing, or at best little, to the achievement of orgasm. One of the effects of the approaching climax is to lessen control of our thoughts and speech, and the woman may say something like 'Deeper, deeper!' absolutely undeliberately; or when the man has failed to satisfy the demands of these sensations she may make some little sound of irritation or annoyance, again quite without meaning to. But men are so sensitive on this point that they are only too quick to interpret such exclamations as criticisms of their essential manhood, with results that can be disastrous in their approach to future relations, since their confidence in their capacity as lovers may be seriously undermined.

All this, I am afraid, has been an unexpected development of the modern attitude of the man's responsibilities towards his wife during love-making. The dictum that the woman has as much right as the man to experience orgasm has been interpreted by the man to mean that he is responsible for her achieving the experience. This has added, in the man's mind, a further significance to his penis and its performance, the inadequacy of which – and hence his failure or success as a lover – he gauges by his ability to 'satisfy his partner'. If his partner, for one reason or another which may be quite unconnected with his technique, fails to achieve orgasm, he holds himself entirely responsible. (This is why young men who experience premature ejaculation are so disproportionately upset by it.) Her failure to achieve orgasm he regards as a reflection on his manhood as represented in his mind by his penis and its performance; and if there is the added implied reflection on the adequacy of the size of his penis, it is an even more terrible blow to his sexual self-respect.

My view is that if the woman has equal rights to experience orgasm this promotes her to equal partnership in the complete sexual relationship. Equal partnership carries with it, however, equal responsibilities for the woman in the achievement of her orgasm, and one of these responsibilities is that she should take care to do or say nothing to injure the sexual self-respect of her partner.

Rather, until he has come to accept the fact of equal partnership and is content to allow the woman to take the initiative in starting love-making and in conducting foreplay, while he remains comparatively passive, she must do everything she can to encourage and even increase his sexual self-respect. To guard against unintentional words, sounds or actions is one way – a negative way. On the positive side she should leave her partner in no doubt that his penis occupies a special place in her sexual affections. She should flatter it with the attentions she pays to it, and she can bestow praise upon it obliquely by expressing her pleasure at the satisfaction she is receiving or has received from its activity in actual love-making. I shall later say briefly how she can do this, but I have introduced it at this point because probably at no other point in love-making except in the immediate after-glow of orgasm do the physical and the psychological become so inextricably intertwined as in the man's regard for his penis and its performance.

Unlike you, your partner is said to have no secondary sexual organs. Strictly speaking, this is true; but there are some men whose nipples, and particularly the right one, are as responsive to fondling with the fingers or mouth as yours are. The man's breasts are not connected to his sexual nervous system as are the woman's, nevertheless quite a number of men admit that the penis can be brought to erection by this fondling.

Generally speaking, these men are highly sensuous – that is, especially responsive to touch in parts of their bodies outside their sexual areas – and their nipples are, for a man's, well-developed. On the other hand, men who are not highly sensuous, but whose nipples are well-developed, have equally admitted to a heightening of tension in their sex organs by the fondling of the nipples, especially with the lips or tongue.

✻   ✻   ✻

This concludes our primary consideration of the male sex organs, but before I leave this description of the physical sexual characteristics, I want to return for a few moments to a further consideration of the properties of the woman's clitoris.

After about three months' development in its mother's womb the baby begins to display certain definite sexual features. It has three openings between its rudimentary legs and a tiny protuberance just above the topmost opening. It is quite impossible to tell whether it is going to be a boy or girl, for it has the sexual characteristics of both. Between the fifth and sixth months it becomes apparent that if it is to be a boy the two upper openings disappear and from now on the protuberance begins to develop rapidly into a miniature penis, while the testicles descend from the lower part of the body, where they have been waiting, and form the scrotal pouch for themselves.

If, however, it is going to be a girl, the three openings remain. Nor does the protuberance disappear, but does, in fact, develop slightly, but only slightly, to form the clitoris.

This being so, it can be readily understood why it is that the clitoris of the mature woman has several characteristics of the man's penis. The little head which appears above the flesh would have been the head had it developed into a penis; and while it has no opening such as the penis has, it is constructed of the same material as the glans penis. Similarly, the shaft which is buried under the flesh would have been the tubular body of the penis. In addition, it possesses erectile qualities, and when the woman is roused it swells a little and hardens. The head also contains much the same kind of mass of super-sensitive nerves as the head of the penis possesses, which are the man's chief orgasm-producing agents.

As the penis is in the man, the clitoris is the most easily stimulated of the woman's sexual apparatus, and its stimulation provides her with the most intense sensations. Gentle rubbing of the head of the clitoris with the fingers or the caress of the partner's tongue or lips, produces orgasm, just as similar applications to the penis produce orgasm for the man.

If you have read and understood what I have written in this chapter you will now be in possession of the essential knowledge of the functioning and capabilities of those organs of yourself and your partner which each of you use in your love-making. Because you have this information you should be able to employ your sex-organs in your physical love-play so that they will function at their best and produce the most intense orgasmic sensations of which they are capable.

And this is one of the major considerations in your making love at all.

3. The Object of Love-making

One of the most important characteristics which differentiates us from animals is our ability to perform the mating act at any time. No other species is capable of doing so. Only when the female animal is carrying an egg ready for fertilization does her physical condition allow her to be penetrated by the male; and only in the presence of a sexually roused female and under the stimulation of her condition is the male himself aroused.

All kinds of stimuli can arouse the male of our species at a few seconds' notice, and the woman's vagina is physically capable of receiving his penis even when she is not sexually roused. But more important still, the woman can be correspondingly roused by a variety of stimuli at any time, *even when she is not carrying an egg capable of fertilization.*

I believe this last to be a very important point to which full weight must be given whenever we are considering the rights and wrongs of contraception. The very fact that our creator has made it possible for us to participate fully and satisfactorily in intercourse when we cannot possibly conceive is, for me, the clearest possible indication that we are meant to use our sexual powers for something other than reproducing our species.

It is as if we are being told: You should use love-making as a means of achieving more than just obedience to your maternal and paternal instincts. Here is a way that you can demonstrate that besides desiring to be mothers and fathers you are also men and women in love with one another. Indeed, we should be fantastically, if not impossibly, dumb if we did not realize that our relationship involved much more than being mothers and fathers. We cannot, in fact, be good parents unless we are good partners; and we cannot be good partners unless we love each other.

Since love is an abstract quality, we can only demonstrate it in our behaviour to one another. The object of all such demonstrations, whether in displays of tenderness or thoughtfulness for the other partner, or in affording him aid and comfort, is to impress upon him that in all possible respects you are 'at one' with him. Fortunately, you have been provided with the means to demonstrate this to him more undeniably clearly than by any other means in actually joining yourself to him physically in sexual intercourse.

There is nothing we can do to give visible and tangible expression to our love which has more chance of imparting our message than love-making.

Very well, then. We have received the signal that we may make love at times when a child cannot possibly be conceived. Such times, however, are of short duration and are periodic. There are several days in between on which a child can be conceived; but does this mean that on these days, however much we may feel the *mental* urge to do so, we are *not* to be allowed to express our love through intercourse, the most convincing means of doing so?

If this were our creator's intention, then it would mean that what was given with one hand is being taken away with the other, and it would be imposing upon us conditions which are impossible for anyone to achieve.

Love cannot be turned on and off like a tap; it is a continuous flow of emotional sensation. And if it cannot be turned off at will, neither can the need to express it be limited to certain times of the month.

Are we then to stifle the desire to express our love at all times when it is not possible to have intercourse without incurring parenthood?

✻   ✻   ✻

The Roman Catholic Church takes a firm and unequivocal stand on its moral interpretation of the control of conception by mechanical means. It fully recognizes that the conception of children is not the sole end of intercourse by stating that it is permissible to participate during the so-called 'safe period'. Indeed it states specifically that the use of the 'safe period' is absolutely unobjectionable on religious-ethical grounds as a means of contraception. It goes even further, and by implication raises no objections either to a certain method of birth-control which employs no mechanical means.

We are therefore posed the question: 'Are we only to make love when we have the mental urge to do so?' which leads us to the undeniable fact that the sex urge has a powerfully physical quality. This is clearly demonstrated by the fact that men and women who are not in love, experience a state of sexual arousal equally as strong as the state experienced by those who are.

In animals the sexual act is a purely physical act, performed by instinct under the stimulus of a physical condition. Because we are rational beings, capable of love and affection, we are able to transform the purely ephemeral physical experience into one of lasting and deep mental significance.

So while it is imperative for us, with our faculty to love, to use sexual intercourse as a visible expression of our feelings – otherwise in this aspect of our lives we reduce ourselves to the animal level – nevertheless it is absolutely impossible for us to ignore the physical side of intercourse; and for the following reason.

There can be no half-measures in love; it must be the whole thing or not at all. How many times do you say to your partner 'I adore you!' and hear him say the same thing to you? If you love your husband to the point of adoration, how are you going to try to prove it to him by the medium of your love-making? Surely only by making the climax of your love-making an unforgetable physical experience each time it happens. But if you are to do this, then in your love-making you must concentrate on the physical capabilities of the sexual parts of yours and your partner's bodies.

In other words, every time you make love your main

objective must be so to act that you achieve the most intense physical response.

If there is any objection to this statement of mine, let me say this – every man and every woman who has taken the trouble to learn what his or her body will do sexually and has brought skill in physical love-making to a high degree of perfection will tell you unhesitatingly that the experience of the really intense orgasm, and particularly its aftermath, brings a sense of intimacy and affection and love for the partner which was never experienced in the time when the love-making did not call upon the fullest physical sexual response from the bodies of the partners.

In the human being's sexual experience of love the physical and the intellectual are undeniably so interrelated that it is impossible for this not to happen. Indeed, if we have not had any conscious experience of it ourselves, plenty of evidence is produced for us daily to show us that this is so. Psychiatrists and Divorce Court judges know that incomplete physical sexual satisfaction produces a mental and intellectual state which in time leads to the complete destruction of love and affection, and opens up the route to the Divorce Court more often than any other cause.

The experience of sexual satisfaction induces just the right atmosphere of physical and mental well-being for affection and love to flourish at their brightest and best. Probably nothing else that we can do *for* our bodies can produce the nervous equilibrium which the mind must have to function properly as can the achievement of sexual satisfaction; and, conversely, nothing we can do can upset our nervous system more rapidly and impair our mental equilibrium than incomplete sexual satisfaction. Read all the books about sex that you can lay your hands on, and you will find repeated in every one of them what I have just said.

To recapitulate briefly, love-making is composed of two inseparable constituents, the intellectual and the physical. The intellectual cannot be attained except through the physical. Further, the intensity of the intellectual experience depends upon the degree of intensity of the physical experience in such a way that the most intense physical experience draws forth the most intense intellectual response.

Thus the physical is the practical means by which the intellectual is achieved.

If care is taken to induce the highest physical response, the highest intellectual response will follow.

Since you are using sexual intercourse as a means of expressing your love for your partner (i.e., the intellectual response) and you want your partner to know that your love for him is deep, you must see to it that you are able to achieve the most intense physical experience in orgasm for him and for yourself that it is possible to achieve.

From this point on, therefore, I shall treat almost exclusively of the physical techniques of love-making.

4. There Must Be No Fear

Between the man and the woman who have decided to demonstrate as fully as they can through love-making the depth of their love for one another there exist no such things as modesty and immodesty.

Before I can explain what I mean by this I must refer briefly to the subject of sexual perversion. There are individuals who can only achieve orgasm by the infliction of physical pain by others upon them (masochists) or by them upon others (sadists), and there are others who are known as fetishists, who can be sexually aroused by seeing their partners dressed in a certain way, or wearing one particular garment or more; or are capable of reaching orgasm only if they themselves are wearing certain articles of clothing. Apart from such unnatural requirements for the inducement of arousal or orgasm, there is nothing which men and women who are partners in a sexual relationship can do with one another which can be stigmatized as 'wrong'.

This is what I mean when I say that modesty and immodesty do not exist in love-making between the sexually normal man and woman. Once they have decided to give themselves to one another there is nothing shameful or of 'bad taste' in anything they do to one another. Indeed, if they are to come anywhere near to achieving the fullest possible satisfaction from orgasm they must give themselves fully, without holding back of any kind at any stage of the love-making. No part of their bodies must be withheld from the sight or touch of their partner; and if the contact of *any* part of their bodies with the sexual parts of their partner produces heightened sensations, then such contact must not be denied to their partner. And whatever they may do in this respect, they must accept that they are behaving normally, with absolute right.

I cannot stress too strongly that neither you nor your partner can hope to achieve the greatest measure of success – which is our aim in this book – without entering upon and conducting your love-making with complete abandon. This may raise problems for those whose upbringing makes abandon difficult. This means that there must be no reservations of any kind, that your mental attitude must be complementary to your physical behaviour.

*   *   *

As reservations are seated in the mind, this brings us to consider one of the most common and one of the strongest mental barriers which obstruct completely uninhibited physical behaviour and the way in which this barrier can be broken down.

The barrier is the fear of conception. Fear of conception is more responsible than any other factor in preventing the woman particularly from attaining our objective – the most intense orgasm of which she is capable. In many women, who are not well acquainted with the methods by which the possibility of conception can be removed, this fear can cause a fear of sexual intercourse which in extreme cases can prevent any sexual arousal whatsoever. Almost certainly such a degree of fear will reflect upon the man if he insists upon intercourse, so that in time his woman grows afraid of him and ceases to have any feelings of love for him at all.

One of our first objects, then, must be the complete removal of the cause of such fear. This can be done by employing some reliable method of contraception. But there are reliable methods which have other drawbacks to the achievement of full abandonment. If we are to employ a contraceptive we must employ the one which is reliable in its contraceptive function and at the same time allows intercourse to be carried out with the least interference with the natural sequence of coital actions.

The principle of all contraceptive methods is to prevent the sperm from reaching the egg, and this can be done in eight main ways:

(a) by the method known as coitus interruptus (which is tacitly accepted by the Roman Catholic Church, since no mechanical device is used);

(b) by the method known as the Safe Period or Rhythm Method (which is also permitted by the Roman Catholic Church for the same reason);

(c) by the man covering his penis with a sheath which prevents the sperm from being ejaculated into the vagina;

(d) by inserting into the vagina substances which will kill the sperms immediately they come into contact with them, but which, at the same time, do not harm the woman;

(e) by the woman obstructing the opening of the womb by a device which is impenetrable by the sperms;

(f) by having fitted an Intra-Uterine Device (IUD, coil, loop) which prevents conception by stopping the fertilized egg from attaching itself to the lining of the womb;

(g) by sterilization: vasectomy for men and tying off the Fallopian tubes for women;

(h) the contraceptive Pill.

*   *   *

In coitus interruptus no mechanical device or spermicidal substance is used by the man or the woman. It consists of the man withdrawing his penis from the vagina shortly before orgasm and ejaculation occur.

Let me say at once that coitus interruptus is *not only the most unreliable of any method of birth control, but it is also definitely harmful.* This is not merely my opinion, it is the considered and strongly held opinion of all doctors well versed in these matters and of all other experts in sexual practice and behaviour.

It is unreliable because minute quantities of semen are exuded from the penis before orgasm takes place – particularly is this true when the degree of arousal is high and the erection is very strong – and the man is absolutely unaware of such emissions. If this has happened, he might just as well not bother to withdraw at all, but deposit the whole of the ejaculate into the vagina. As I have already said, each ejaculate of semen contains between 250,000,000 and 400,000,000 sperms. In each of the minute quantities which the occasional muscular throbbing of the excited penis may expel there may be only 200 sperms. But whether 200 or 400,000,000 are deposited in the vagina, only one is required to fertilize the egg.

It is usual practice when the penis is withdrawn in coitus interruptus for the man to continue to lie upon his partner and to complete his orgasm by moving the penis against her pubic bone and lower stomach. In many cases, even where the penis is of average size, and particularly when it is below average, some of the semen may be deposited near the entrance to the vagina. Such is the power of movement of the sperms and the state of lubrication of the inner lips that once the sperms make contact with the smooth and slippery surface of the small lips, in no time at all they are heading for the vaginal entrance, taking that direction with unerring instinct.

It is not widely appreciated that the semen need not be deposited in the vagina for the sperms to find their way to the womb. There are on record cases of young women who have become pregnant though their hymens were still intact, which meant that the vagina had never received the penis. Such cases, which have occurred in the past only rarely, are nowadays becoming more and more frequent among young women who indulge in what is known as 'heavy petting'.

In 'heavy petting' every phase and type of love-play is indulged in, but the penis is never inserted into the vagina. Orgasm is either reached by the action of the male I have just described, or by a far more dangerous practice. Recognizing the girl's right to experience orgasm, as the climax approaches the boy places himself above the girl, and while she exposes her clitoris by holding back the lips with her fingers he (or sometimes she) stimulates it with the head of the penis until orgasm in both is reached. The penile stimulation of the clitoris in this way is the most effective of all methods of clitoral stimulation, and the deposition of the semen directly upon the clitoris while the penis continues to rub gently against it practically never fails to produce almost simultaneous orgasm.

Since simultaneous orgasm by the man and woman is regarded by many to be a highly desired form of climax to intercourse – I shall be speaking of the various aspects of orgasm in the next chapter – some couples who have discovered this way of producing it practise it from time to time as an alternative method of reaching orgasm. If the woman is using a contraceptive there is nothing to be said against it; but if the couple are practising coitus interruptus, they are literally asking for the woman to become pregnant.

Or again, the man may misjudge the speed at which his climax is approaching and fail to withdraw his penis until ejaculation has started. If only the first spurt of semen is deposited inside the vagina, they are a very lucky couple indeed if the woman does not become pregnant. You may think that the occasions upon which the man misjudges the speed of his approaching climax are rare, but it is not so. You do not need to be told by me that in the process of achieving orgasm there is a 'point of no return'. The contractions of the vaginal muscles, which play a very large role in inducing orgasm, reach a certain pitch at which nothing, absolutely nothing, that you can do can stop them from gathering impetus, the inevitable conclusion of which is the explosion of orgasm. Similarly in the man, the muscles which are responsible for forcing the semen out of the penis by their contractions, having reached a certain pitch in their movements, cannot be quietened until orgasm has taken place. The degree of violence with which these muscles react can vary from intercourse to intercourse in the same man, and it is quite possible for him not to appreciate how strong it actually is on certain given occasions.

I think I have said enough to demonstrate how very unreliable coitus interruptus is as a contraceptive method. In addition, however, it is about as unsatisfactory from other points of view as it is unreliable; and from the unsatisfactory aspects spring the harmful results.

Let us examine what happens to a couple practising coitus interruptus. They indulge in love-play as the means of bringing each other to a state of arousal which will culminate in orgasm. At a certain point the man inserts his penis for the final stage of the intercourse. If it were a normal intercourse, the man would retain his penis in the vagina until both had reached orgasm, by means of penile movements against the vaginal walls and clitoral stimulation. The man practising coitus interruptus makes the same movements, then just as the climax is about to break he withdraws his penis.

Now, the actual acts of insertion and withdrawal of the penis produce special sensations in both partners. However strong the man's erection may be, the sensation produced by the penis being caressed by the entrance to the vagina almost invariably causes more blood to flow into the cavities of the penis, thus further enlarging it, with accompanying highly pleasurable sensations. Withdrawal of the penis, if made quickly, while it is still erect causes a sudden, if very slight, diminution in size, and the sensations caused by this rapid decrease in high tension produce a corresponding diminution in satisfaction and slightly unpleasant sensations.

For the woman the sensations accompanying insertion and withdrawal of the penis, while of the same quality, are much more intense. As I shall be explaining later, it is a useful technique in the arousal of the woman for the man to insert his penis earlier than he and his partner might usually feel was the appropriate time, and then after a few minutes of repose to withdraw completely, wait four or five seconds, and then re-insert, repeating the technique half a dozen times or so. If the greatest care is taken to withdraw the penis, and particularly the head, very, very slowly, the deleterious sensations of a rapid withdrawal are avoided, and the rhythms of the arousal of both, but especially the woman, are enhanced.

The sensations set up by the urgent and sometimes clumsy withdrawal of the penis just at this stage of love-making cannot fail to impair the intensity of the orgasm both for the man and the woman. In fact, they may completely throw the woman off balance, and she may be unable to reach her orgasm at all. She is then left in a very uncomfortable state of high nervous tension which makes her extremely irritable, with her nerves on edge. If this happens frequently it will not be long before she is thinking how very unfair it all is. It is all right for her partner, he gets what he wants; but just as she is thinking she is going to be satisfied, all possibility of satisfaction is suddenly snatched away. Only a comparatively short period will elapse before the physical condition in which she is left by the non-achievement of orgasm in organs highly congested by the physical results of a high state of desire – and the mental attitude which almost inevitably complements this physical state – will induce functional derangements of the nervous system, with corresponding bad mental reactions.

I have already briefly referred, in Chapter 2, to the sensations that most women feel, as the point-of-no-return approaches, for deeper and deeper penetration of the penis. If, by the position that is adopted for intercourse, actual deeper penetration can be achieved by the man, or he has been able to create the illusion of deeper penetration (I shall be explaining later how this may be done), the sensation can go a very long way to bringing about orgasm, even if it does not actually provoke its achievement, which in some cases it is capable of doing on its own. If the penis is withdrawn at the time when the woman is desperately hoping for its deeper penetration, the psychological effects and the physical results which I have just described are almost certain to occur.

From this you will see that coitus interruptus has absolutely nothing to recommend it as a reliable method of contraception and has a very great deal against it on physical and psychological grounds.

It certainly cannot help to create the complete absence of fear which we have agreed is one of the most essential requirements for satisfactory love-making. On the contrary, it is almost certain to invoke fear.

Yet it is one of the most common practices – chiefly, I think, because it costs nothing and neither man nor woman has the inclination to treat their love-making seriously.

If you and your partner have been using coitus interruptus I implore you to stop at once, and to employ one of the mechanical devices, one of the most commonly used being the sheath worn by the man.

*   *   *

The next method, especially advocated by the Roman Catholic Church, and one that employs no mechanical device, is the Safe Period or Rhythm Method, which is based on the woman's menstrual cycle.

The ripening of the egg and its discharge – known as ovulation – usually takes place about half-way between the completion of the last menstrual period and the beginning of the next. The egg must be fertilized within a comparatively short time of ovulation, otherwise it dies.

If a woman has a normal menstrual cycle of twenty-eight days, she is, therefore, according to this reckoning, fertile only on the fifteenth day before her next period is due to begin. But as the male sperm can live up to forty-eight hours inside the woman, any sperm deposited on the seventeenth and sixteenth days before menstruation may also fertilize the egg.

Accordingly, therefore, on the seventeenth, sixteenth and fifteenth days before menstruation is due to begin the woman is most capable of conceiving. On all other days she should be incapable of becoming pregnant – in other words, may be considered 'safe'.

But it is difficult to know the exact moment of ovulation, so to be quite sure (in theory), the fourteenth and thirteenth days (i.e. the two after the calculated date of ovulation) are also put out of bounds, so to speak.

Those who advocate this method add yet another two days on either side in order to increase the margin of safety, making the period when the woman is *unsafe* stretch from the twenty-first to the eleventh days before the completion of the next menstrual period.

To give a concrete example: A woman begins to menstruate on 1 February, and because she has a twenty-eight day cycle she can expect to begin menstruating again on 28 February or

1 March. Counting back fifteen days from this date, she should ovulate on 13 February. To be sure she is safe, she adds two more days on either side, and refrains from intercourse from 10 February to 18 February. If she has a period which lasts five days, she may then consider herself 'safe' from 6 to 9 February (four days) and from 19 to 27 February (nine days), though the supercareful reduce this last period by another three days, making her 'safe' period ten days in her twenty-eight-day menstrual cycle.

Note: the counting must begin at the day on which the next menstruation is expected to go *backwards*, not from the last day of bleeding of the last menstruation and forwards.

This is the theory; but the Safe Period relies for its success entirely upon the absolute regularity of the woman's menstrual cycle, and you do not need me to tell you that though a woman's menstrual cycle may be quite regular, month after month, for many years, it is likely to become irregular without any warning. Since the woman cannot know that she has become irregular until she finds herself menstruating before or after the normal date, she cannot know when ovulation has taken place; and if she cannot know this, she cannot calculate her 'safe' days with certainty, even with the help of the charts and calculating gadgets which are now available.

There is a good deal of evidence to show that this method provides a very small measure of protection against conception, and I would strongly advise my non-Catholic readers to have nothing at all to do with it.

If it works, admittedly it has none of the ill-effects of coitus interruptus, since full intercourse is performed, the man reaching orgasm while his penis remains in the vagina and he can assure that the woman reaches hers; but unless you can be absolutely sure it is going to work reliably – and of this you certainly cannot be – there will always be fear of pregnancy.

*   *   *

The sheath, or 'french letter', is made of very thin but at the same time very strong latex. It is bought rolled in such a way that by placing it over the head of the penis it can easily be slipped down until it covers the whole length of the penis. The prices differ slightly according to make.

Manufacturers have been successfully experimenting in the last few years in the production of sheaths which, when in position, are as undetectable as possible and interfere with sensation as little as possible. Sheaths are now on the market which are so light – and therefore so thin – that the weight of them cannot be felt when they are held in the hand. They are also treated with various lubricants and in some cases, spermicides to further increase their reliability.

Nowadays, the manufacture of sheaths has reached such a stage of perfection that though they are much thinner than they used to be they are also much stronger, so that the possibility that they may tear in use or may contain tiny holes through which the sperm might escape is almost nil. From a practical point of view, therefore, the sheath represents a very high degree of reliability – almost, but not quite, one hundred per cent.

Many husbands and wives, particularly after a really intense orgasm, like to remain coupled until all the actual orgasmic sensations have disappeared, which usually only happens when the swelling of the woman's vaginal lips and the man's erection have completely subsided.

It is not technically possible, apparently, for a sheath to be made with a sufficient degree of elasticity so that it grips tightly the relaxed penis as well as being able to stretch enough to be capable of being applied to the much larger erect penis. So if the penis is retained in the vagina until erection has subsided one of two things may happen – either the semen may flow backwards under the pressure of the vaginal subsidence and exude from the sheath or the sheath may slip off the penis altogether; in which case, efforts to retrieve it are bound to cause semen to flow out of it into the vagina. Both 'accidents' could result in conception. Many men and women feel that is a defect in the sheath, and that to avoid these accidents the great pleasure of remaining coupled until subsidence of sensations and organs is complete – and, indeed, very great mental advantages accrue from this practice – must be foregone.

In addition, it must be admitted that despite the reliability of the sheath as a contraceptive, its use also has other disadvantages. The woman's vaginal nerves and the orgasm-producing nerves of the penis as well as those situated in the skin covering the body of the penis are so fashioned that they react best when they are in direct contact with one another. If even the thinnest barrier prevents the vaginal nerves from coming into direct contact with the penile nerves much of their sensitivity is lost. The penile nerves are also very sensitive and the slightest constrictive pressure, such as the sheath must exert to stay in position, has the effect of deadening their sensitivity. From one point of view this is probably an advantage, for it helps the man more easily to retard his climax, but the climax, when it comes, is never so intense when a sheath is being worn as when the penis is naked.

Another disadvantage of the sheath is when to put it on. If it is put on at the beginning of the love-play, the woman cannot pay to the penis many of the attentions designed to heighten her partner's pleasure, particularly oral caresses. Besides, its presence forces itself on the attention of both man and woman and introduces an element of artificiality into love-making, which, as we shall see presently, ideally should not be there.

If, on the other hand, the man waits until just before inserting the penis into the vagina before putting on the sheath, the rhythm of the approach to orgasm is interrupted; and though he may quickly make up any leeway lost, the woman, while waiting, may fall so far back that difficulty may be experienced in re-establishing the rhythm before her partner reaches the point-of-no-return. Also, the element of artificiality extrudes itself.

Other than the once-and-for-all step of a vasectomy, which is a simple operation that sterilizes the male, this is the only mechanical device widely available to the man, and it is clearly seen that, though it may present a very high degree of protection from conception, it is far from ideal. Obviously, what is ideally required is a device which, if properly used, assures the very greatest degree of contraception, can be applied before love-making begins, and need not be removed until some hours after intercourse has been completed, and that is absolutely undetectable to both man and woman.

Fortunately there is such a device which can be applied by the woman; or rather it is a combination of two separate devices.

*   *   *

I have said at the beginning of this description of contraceptive methods, that the aim is to prevent the man's sperm from reaching the woman's egg either by killing off the sperm as soon as it enters the vagina or by constructing a barrier across the entrance to the womb which is completely impenetrable by the sperm.

There are available a number of spermicidal chemicals which cause no physical harm to the woman. They are made up into the form of pessaries which are inserted as near to the entrance of the womb as possible. As soon as any sperm comes into contact with the compound it is instantly killed.

Pessaries do their job, but only if properly applied, otherwise they may be as useless as nothing at all. They must be inserted some time before orgasm takes place to allow the base to be melted by the warmth of the vagina so that the spermicide may be freed.

It they are not inserted early enough, then the spermicide cannot act and sperms may reach the egg. If they are not pushed far enough up into the vagina the head of the penis may go through the deposit and spurt the semen out of contact with the spermicide, on the cervix side of it, and conception can take place.

But even if they are inserted properly and melt properly they impose the disadvantage on the woman of not allowing her to be active during preliminary love-play, and the position in which making love can be engaged in is limited to the one. If the wife does not lie on her back from the time she has inserted the pessary it may slip out, unknown either to her or her partner, before it has melted; or if it does not melt properly and she raises her torso at all, either during love-play or for coupling, the melted deposit may trickle out of her vagina, and what is left behind may not be sufficiently strong to act as a spermicide.

Yet another disadvantage is that even if she lies quite passively on her back some of the melted deposit inevitably trickles down to the entrance of the vagina, and if the man is using oral caresses in this area, he will almost certainly find the taste unpleasant.

But besides these practical disadvantages the number of known failures to prevent conception is proportionately high enough for one to be able to say that this method is not sufficiently reliable enough to be recommended.

Another type of contraceptive for the woman's use is a mechanical barrier inserted in the vagina to close the entrance of the womb to the sperm. This type of barrier is known as the cap. There are two kinds of cap: one, known as the cervical cap, fits tightly over the neck of the womb, the other, known as the diaphragm cap, or, more popularly, the Dutch cap, shuts off the entrance to the womb by 'clipping' on to the far side of the cervix at the far end and tucking tightly in behind the pubic bone at the front end.

Both these caps must be fitted by a doctor in the first place, because since no two women are exactly the same inside; and since the cap must fit perfectly, the cervix must be measured for the cervical cap – as must the distance from the far side of the cervix to the pubic bone for the Dutch cap.

Let me dispose of the cervical cap briefly. As a contraceptive it is very reliable, if used with a spermicidal cream. It has, however, two drawbacks, one of which contains the possibility of quite serious physical damage. First, it is much more difficult to fit than the Dutch cap, and unless the woman has longish fingers she may sometimes run the risk of not getting it properly into position, which automatically makes it unreliable. Second, and much more serious, however, is the physical damage that may be done to the cervix, and in some cases to the whole womb, in removing the cap. Because it must fit tightly to the cervix, if it is to carry out its function with a high degree of reliability, it is often quite difficult to dislodge.

Her efforts to do this may cause the woman to pull on the womb, and frequent pullings may cause tears or other damage to the tissues in which the womb is embedded, or, alternatively, the woman may scratch the neck of the cervix and set up inflammation, which may ultimately result in the development of a cervical cyst, causing much discomfort and a surgical operation to remove it; or both may happen. I personally advise against this type of cap.

This leaves the Dutch cap, and here we have the one type of contraceptive which fulfils all the requirements our device must have. It is almost one hundred per cent reliable if certain simple rules are followed; it is undetectable in use by both man and woman; it can be fitted in less than two minutes by the practised woman, and at any time before intercourse takes place; it can be removed very easily, though it must be kept in place for *at least* eight hours after the deposit of semen in the vagina; it is extremely easy to keep clean; it causes no physical derangement.

The Dutch cap, also known as the diaphragm cap, is much larger than the cervical cap. It is a dome of rubber attached to a strong, spring-like rim. When it is inserted, the far end of the rim 'clips' onto the far side of the cervix, and the front part fits into the space behind the pubic bone, which keeps it firmly in place. Once fitted neither partner can feel it.

Like the cervical cap, it is made in a large variety of sizes, and any woman can be sure of a perfect fit provided she consults an expert in the first place. And here I must stress – and I cannot stress it too strongly – that if the woman wishes to become pregnant she will buy a cap from one of the very few firms who sell direct to her. These firms advertise their wares as coming in three sizes – small, medium and large. But how many women are able to say which size they are? In fact, within one size alone there can be very small differences of measurement, each requiring a different cap.

You must consult your doctor. He may be qualified to attend to you himself. If hs is not, he is certain to know a doctor who is qualified, or will be able to put you in touch with the nearest clinic run by the Family Planning Association, where you will find real experts.

This necessity to consult a doctor and to be taught by him how to insert the cap may put some women off. I hope it will not put you off. So many women are consulting their doctors about their day-by-day sex lives nowadays that the embarrassment which used to exist between patient and doctor in the old days, and for which the doctor was to blame in a very high degree, has disappeared.

Go to your doctor and say: 'Doctor, I want to have a Dutch cap fitted', and I am pretty certain that he will smile at you and reply: 'Good. Just let me have a look at you', exactly as he would if you went to him and said: 'Doctor, I have a sore throat', and he replied: 'I see. Open your mouth and let me have a look at it. Say 'ah'.' In twenty minutes, perhaps less, you will be leaving his surgery in possession of a cap which fits you perfectly and the knowledge of how to insert it.

Any reluctance you may feel about consulting a doctor is sheer foolishness, and I sincerely hope that you will not indulge in it. You can take it from me that the physical and mental benefits bestowed on your sex life by the use of a disphragm cap are extraordinary.

Now, the doctor will tell you two things, both of which are extremely important and which you must observe most meticulously. First, he will impress upon you that the cap must not be used without the application of a spermicidal cream, without which you might just as well not use the cap. This cream must be smeared round the rim of the cap and on the inside of the dome. The cream does not perish the rubber of the cap, nor does it melt and trickle down to the vaginal entrance; it, therefore, cannot be an obstacle to oral caresses in this region.

Second, the doctor will tell you that you must go back and see him a few weeks after the cap has been fitted, and thereafter every two years, if you do not have a planned pregnancy before then. The reason for this is, in the first instance, that in the early days of use the cap may cause minute changes in the interior conformation of the vagina. More often than not these changes are so insignificant that the perfect fit of the cap is not affected. On the other hand, it may just happen that they may be such as to prevent the cap from fitting perfectly, and the next size may now be required. Why you must visit him every two years is because all of us change inside as we grow older; though the changes are slow they are constantly taking place; and childbirth invariably enlarges the vagina.

Again let me stress the absolute necessity of making these visits. If you do not, then you might as well throw the cap away for all the safety it will provide for you. But if you will carry out these two simple rules – the application of the spermicide to the cap, and the periodic visits to your doctor or clinic – you need have no fear whatever during your love-making.

*   *   *

There is also the I.U.D. or Coil. This is a plastic or copper device which is inserted in the womb, and prevents an egg from settling in the womb. You must consult your doctor or a Family Planning Clinic. They will warn you of the drawbacks of the I.U.D. such as it slipping out unnoticed.

*   *   *

The contraceptive pill. This form of contraception has made great strides in the last twenty years. There are two types of pill. One is the Combined or Every Day (ED) pill which contains two hormones. Taken regularly it stops the monthly production of the fertile egg (ovulation). From time to time there have been scares about the side-effects of its constant use in some women. To overcome this, there have been constant attempts to produce a Pill which will not produce the side-effects.

Out of these experiments has emerged the Mini-Pill, which contains only one hormone; but it is only 98% efficient, whereas the ED is 100% efficient.

If you are considering using the Pill, you must consult your doctor or a Family Planning Clinic, who will consider your medical history and decide which Pill will be suitable for you.

*   *   *

Finally there is sterilization, which is a permanent form of contraception.

The male version is called vasectomy, and consists of a minor operation in which the sperm ducts leading from the testicles are cut or tied, so that no sperms can get into the ejaculate. It does not interfere with the man's enjoyment of sex. He still has orgasms and ejaculates. But the operation is irreversible.

The female version consists of closing the Fallopian tubes so that active sperms cannot reach the egg. It also is irreversible.

Consult your doctor in both cases.

*   *   *

If you are let down by your contraceptive, some doctors and clinics provide 'Morning After' contraception. But this can only be used in a real emergency. But do make sure that you take the fear out of love-making.

5. The Nature of the Orgasm

I do not believe that the man or woman has yet been born who can exactly or adequately describe just what he or she feels in orgasm. It is a sensation of exquisite physical pleasure, and the more intense it is the more exquisitely pleasurable it is. I shall not attempt to say more than that.

Besides the pleasure which the orgasm provides, it is absolutely essential for the relief of sexual tension. When you become sexually roused your own sex organs, like your partner's penis, swell and become engorged with blood. But this swelling causes only one part of the tension. Nervous sensations are initiated and continue to intensify until granted the outlet of the orgasmic explosion. This is why, though the physical part of you may subside if you do not bring about an orgasm, you still find yourself what is termed 'unsatisfied'. The sensations at this time are of a physical nature and react on the nervous system in such a way that both physical and mental sensations of irritability are experienced.

If one can use an analogy at all, the only commensurable one is that of the volcano. The volcano begins rumbling long before it erupts, but its rumbling and interior movement, from the beginning of the rumbling until the climax of eruption, are one long mounting tension, working always towards that moment when the forces within it become too strong for its containing walls of earth and rock, and it throws up its fire and ashes and its molten lava flows out. Once the interior movement starts it does not finish until eruption has occurred.

In the sexually roused man and woman, once the sexual nervous system has become activated nothing can quieten it except the physical explosion of the orgasm. At least, that is how it seems. Actually, what happens in orgasm is extremely complex and, for the lay mind, difficult to understand. But if you are aware of the fact that the sensations of sexual arousal can *only* be quietened by orgasm this is sufficient knowledge of what happens and what is necessary before body and mind can return to normal.

The greater the degree of physical sensation in orgasm, the more soothed the nervous system is, and the greater the sense of mental satisfaction. It is logical, then, that the object of love-making should be to produce the greatest intensity of orgasmic sensation that it is possible to achieve. But to be able to do this a certain know-how is required.

It is thought by very many people, though I am not absolutely convinced of it, that if the man and woman 'come', as we describe orgasm in ordinary language, at the same moment, this simultaneous 'coming' provides the maximum of pleasurable sensation that it is possible for that particular woman and that particular man to achieve from orgasm. There is a good deal in this idea, but many men testify that they have the most intense sensations if they come fifteen or thirty seconds *after* their partners, and the women of these men testify that they also experience their most intense sensations in these conditions. They say that when they reach their orgasm the actual explosion may not be of maximum intensity, but that the thrusting movements of the penis, which the men invariably make at this point to bring himself off, prolong the period of maximum sensations, and that when the man spurts his semen into them the intensity of sensation is increased so that they appear to have – and quite likely do have – a second orgasm.

       ✻   ✻   ✻

A second orgasm in so short a time? How can that happen? The positive answer lies in one of the fundamental sexual differences between the male and the female.

I have said earlier that any normal healthy man can be sexually roused, have a strong erection and achieve orgasm in about two minutes. The women in the world who could claim a similar period for the complete process are probably one in a million. It is not enough for the woman to feel the desire to make love to bring her to a state of physical arousal; and her sexual nervous system needs far longer encouragement to reach the climax than any man could possibly tolerate.

It is because of this considerable difference in the tempo between the man and the woman that a definite technique of love-play is required to bring them both to a successful conclusion – a technique which is designed to slow down the speed of the man's rush towards climax at the same time that it stimulates the woman to move faster towards hers.

Let us consider what is required for the man to achieve his orgasm. No matter how intense his desire may be, his orgasm will not occur unless the nerves are stimulated in some way by physical means. (The possible exception to this is in the experience of the erotic dream, though it has been observed that in quite a large number of cases even in dreams there is unconscious manipulation of the penis by the hands or the thrusting of the penis against the bed covers.) The natural means is by moving his penis against the vaginal walls, and the delicate membranes of the vagina have the power to stimulate the orgasm-producing nerves to bring him off, requiring between two and four minutes, provided he inserts his penis at the moment full erection is achieved, and he has taken part in no pre-penetration stimulation.

The woman also requires physical stimulation to achieve her orgasm. Unlike the man, however, the orgasm-producing nerves are not concentrated in one spot, and in addition, though the vaginal walls are able to stimulate the orgasm-producing nerves of the penis to orgasm, and though they are supplied with nerves which produce sensations in her, these nerves are much less erotically charged. So gentle are they in their reactions, in fact, that except for a very few women, as I have said earlier, it is practically certain that no amount of penile stimulation alone will induce the achievements of orgasm.

Without doubt a woman's most sensitive erotic nerves are situated in her clitoris. She can produce orgasm by stimulating these nerves alone; but even if an effective instrument of stimulation – either the head of her partner's penis, or his tongue, or lips, or fingers – is applied, it still requires ten to fifteen minutes of uninterrupted stimulation to bring her off.

Nor is she slower merely because her orgasm-producing nerves require longer stimulation. From the moment stimulation by any means is applied to the penis, the man's progress towards orgasm is a sharp and rapid upwards rush. But even if the woman is uninterruptedly stimulated and the effectiveness of the method remains steady or increases, she approaches her orgasm by a series of steps.

Again, the blindingly ecstatic sensations of orgasm in the man are experienced by him for four or five seconds only. Fortunately this is long enough to grant him absolute physical and mental relief. But the moment the peak explosion of orgasmic sensation is experienced all sensations of an orgasmic character fade in an even shorter time than it took him to come off. The woman, on the other hand, has a longer experience of the climax – between ten to fifteen seconds – and the sensations subside much more slowly, so that some minutes after the first explosion of orgasm she is still experiencing orgasmic sensations, while pleasurable sensations continue for some minutes further still. So it can be said that if greater effort and patience are required for the woman to come off, the patience and effort are well compensated by the results.

Yet another orgasmic difference between male and female is that within a few minutes of the man's coming even the strongest erection may have completely subsided and there must be a pause of at least twenty minutes before the penis can be re-stimulated into erection. If another orgasm is now attempted – and the impulses of the new erection are generally very strongly insistent that this should occur – the *shortest* time needed for stimulation to orgasm will be fifteen minutes, while often twenty to thirty minutes are needed, and the orgasm, while not being quite so explosive, is nevertheless very intense and of much longer duration.

✻   ✻   ✻

The desire and ability to achieve more than one orgasm – from the same act for women, and from different acts following closely upon one another for men – are closely connected with what is known as the sexual urge, and this, too, we must consider briefly, because it is essential for us to know what our potentials and requirements are before we can extract from love-making to orgasm the greatest possible satisfaction.

One person is placid, another highly excited; one is highly intelligent, another not an intellectual type; one is slow to anger, another is easily provoked to rage; one has a bright and happy disposition, another is taciturn and morbid. The variety of human characteristics, differentiating one individual from the next, is almost limitless, and this differentiation is carried into sexual characterization.

The sexual 'character' falls into three main types, which apply equally to men and women, and are classified thus: the highly-sexed (or passionate), the medium-sexed, and the lowly-sexed. These classifications are roughly based on what is known as the frequency of the sexual urge. The medium-sexed, who form by far the largest group of men and women and can therefore be said to represent the norm, experience sexual desire, arousal and the need for orgasm two or three times in a week (in their twenties an average of four times); the lowly-sexed may experience sexual desire, arousal and the need for orgasm only once a fortnight, or once a month; while the highly-sexed have a daily urge, and often a twice- or thrice-daily urge.

To the medium-sexed and the lowly-sexed it may come as a surprise to find that there are men and women who feel such a frequent urge as this last. I think all of us have had sufficient experience to realize that there are people whose interest in sex appears to be one of their predominant features. I have a shrewd suspicion, too, that we rather disapprove of such people. We are inclined to interpret their high sexuality as being an unhealthy interest in sex which they make no attempt to control, but, on the contrary, stimulate and encourage their desire for sexual activity, the means for achieving which they often seem to go out of their way to discover. In other words, they make no attempt at self-control, as we put it.

In much the same way, and this is particularly true of men, we are apt to despise the lowly-sexed. Their apparent disinterest in sex seems to us to display a lack of manhood and womanhood, making of them creatures belonging almost to a sub-species.

We are wrong to condemn either the highly-sexed or the lowly-sexed, and if we do think like this, it shows very clearly that we are quite ignorant of the nature of the sexual urge and the varying degrees of sexuality which different people possess.

The sexual urge is as valid a characteristic of a man or a woman as are fair hair and beautiful large brown eyes, or even temper and quick wit. It is an essential component of a person's total make-up, and can no more be ignored or changed than can any other physical or psychological characteristic. It is the result of activities of certain *physical* parts of our bodies – secretions and the glands that make them – and not of any psychological reaction. In the highly-sexed these glands are extremely active, and thereby cause frequent sexual arousal; and the highly-sexed cannot be blamed for this. A low activity of the same glands is responsible for the low frequency of arousal, and similarly the lowly-sexed cannot be blamed for the infrequency of their urge.

Now, the highly-sexed, besides requiring frequent experience of orgasm, require also a highly intense orgasmic sensation to achieve relief, or, alternatively, have need of multiple orgasm to be completely satisfied. Naturally enough, they are capable of achieving highly intensive orgasms and quickly repeated orgasms, and are equipped with the requisite sexual physical ability – that is, the ability to promote frequent strong and full erection in the man, and physical arousal, a state known as tumescence, in the woman – to satisfy their needs.

In addition, the highly-sexed come much more quickly. This is a great advantage to the woman, but it calls for a very strict control from the man, who, if he were medium-sexed, would still need only a very brief period of stimulation to reach his climax. It is very rare indeed to find a highly-sexed man or woman who does not appreciate the quality of the demands made by his or her sexuality; and as a consequence you will find that such people are completely free of inhibitions in their love-making activities. They abandon themselves to the dictates of the rhythm of their arousal far more easily than the medium-sexed, and achieve the intensity of sensation and high degree of satisfaction far more frequently than those who are medium-sexed but who do not employ the carefully-thought-out and executed technique of love-making essential to the medium-sexed man. In effect, despite the fact that they may be regarded by their more normal fellows as being obsessed with sex, and despite the fact that sex may often seem to themselves to be somewhat of a burden – even if well matched with a partner of similar sexuality it is not always possible for reasons of work, or lack of opportunity, to go to bed each time the urge becomes demanding – they are somewhat to be envied.

Nor have we any justification for despising the lowly-sexed. Contrary to what we may think, the way they are endowed with sex does not deprive them of anything. The men are capable of strong erections and equally capable of sustaining erection for a sufficient time to allow them to achieve orgasm; and though the intensity of their orgasm may not be half that achieved by the medium-sexed, it is sufficient to give them complete relief and full satisfaction, for their less demanding needs are proportionately easily met.

A certain problem does arise, however, supposing a highly-sexed woman makes love to a lowly-sexed man. She needs intercourse with a frequency which it is extremely difficult for him to meet physically and there is very little he can do about it, unless he is prepared to co-operate with his lover in techniques of stimulation which will bring her to orgasm without him being sexually physically implicated. But such techniques can become repugnant to him, and they certainly do not satisfy the woman to the degree which her sexuality demands.

In the converse case, of the highly-sexed man making love

to a lowly-sexed woman, a similar problem arises. A pro-
gramme of artificial stimulation is not so necessary here, since
the woman is capable of allowing the penis to penetrate her
when she is not in a physically roused condition. Nevertheless,
persistent intercourse when it is not wanted inevitably creates
all kinds of reactions, which can ultimately kill desire altogether.
Instinct, if allowed to operate, can reveal such violently
opposed sexualities, and any relationship which is capable of
turning into love should be abandoned before love can
develop.

With regard to the highly-sexed man making love to the
medium-sexed woman, and to the converse case, I personally
do not believe that any problem need arise, provided the
incompatibility is recognized and appreciated, and an intelligent
approach is made to it, with a degree of give and take on both
sides. The so-called medium-sexed woman is capable of
much more frequent activity than her classification seems to
denote, and she can go a very long way towards meeting the
needs of a highly-sexed man if she is prepared to overcome an
initial natural reluctance to allow herself to be roused at times
when she feels no sex urge at all. More than half this reluctance
is psychological in origin, for if subjected to a highly efficient
technique of love-making the woman can, in fact, be as easily
roused as any man, and the results can leave nothing to be
desired.

A great deal is made by some experts and specialists of the
'moodiness of women'. While, admittedly, an extreme reluctance to make love – to the point of refusing to do so – has
physical reasons at times, especially at the approach of
menstruation, in the general run of things it is the effect of an
ingrained psychological attitude of which the woman may not
be conscious, for it is a legacy handed down from her Victorian
ancestors. This attitude is really a defence-mechanism designed
by the Victorian woman's fear of frequent pregnancy, disgust
with sex arising out of her total, or almost total, lack of
orgasmic experience, and the peculiar idea that if she lets her
partner make love to her every time he wants to she will make
herself 'cheap'. While I can feel some sympathy with the first
two reasons, the last reason strikes me as being unbelievably

foolish. She is not selling herself to her partner, not even giving herself, but *sharing* herself; and whoever heard of one partner in a shared experience being 'cheap'? In fact, it is impossible without the other partner also being 'cheap', and if both are cheap they won't realize it.

Mind you, the highly-sexed man must be prepared to contribute something, too. He should remember that he has a ready means of relieving his physical condition, and from time to time he should make use of masturbation, accepting the fact that he must forgo the intense pleasure which accompanies orgasm in intercourse for an experience which is a pale image of the real thing. But if he will look upon it not as a sexual experience but merely as a physical necessity, he will not find the sacrifice too great, nor will he develop any psychological difficulties. The wife, too, can do much to help him – for it is he whose needs are insistent, who must be helped, not she – if she herself will bring about his relief in this way. It is merely a matter of two or three minutes' duration; but to have her do it more than doubles the climactic results which he would achieve if he attended to it himself.

While I am on this point, I would like to say that there is absolutely nothing against partners bringing each other off without intercourse. There are occasions when the love-play produces sensations so highly pleasurable that it would be foolish to interrupt the rhythm of them merely to assume positions for the normal conclusion of the intercourse. In fact, if the couple did break off what they were doing to allow the man to insert his penis, by the time he had done so the quality of the sensations would probably have disappeared and could not be recaptured; in which event the intensity of the orgasm then achieved by intercourse would only have a fraction of the intensity of the orgasm which would have been experienced if the stimulation had been continued to climax without intercourse.

There is nothing perverted in such activity, nor in the fact of an orgasm achieved in this way. If it were practised in preference to penetration always, it would become a perversion; but as a natural occurrence it happens only rarely that sensations of this particular quality – which I will not attempt to describe; they are easily recognized – are induced. I mention it, because it does occasionally give rise to some anxiety in partners who get the idea that the sensations are not natural simply because the climax is not achieved by the usual means.

Or again, the man may stimulate his partner in such a way as to induce in her an unusually rapid progress towards orgasm. He produces in her, by the method of stimulation he is using, sensations which again it would be foolish to prevent from gathering impetus to the point of climax. This being so, he brings her off, while he does not come himself. If he then inserts his penis immediately after the climax of her orgasm has been achieved, and while her orgasmic sensations are still relatively powerful, and brings himself off by a series of strong and rapid intra-vaginal thrusts, he is very likely to induce in her a second, or even a third, peak of orgasmic sensation in a short space of time, which allows her the deepest satisfaction. At the same time, under the stimulus of her behaviour, which will be quite involuntary, his own orgasmic sensations will match hers in intensity, even though he has had only one orgasm to her two or three. There is nothing wrong or unnatural about this either.

It is also possible for a medium-sexed man to adjust himself to a highly-sexed woman; and indeed it is far easier for him to do so. All medium-sexed husbands are capable of arousal at any time and can derive unfailing relief from any encounter. If there is any reluctance to co-operate at any time, this reluctance also has psychological origins; though exactly how they have come into being, or what the nature of them is, it is not easy to say. I think, generally speaking, they arise from the fact that men have been conditioned to believing themselves to be the sole *active* partner in sex, and when they find themselves matched with women demanding more frequent activity than their own sex-urge prompts in them they feel that their role is being usurped, and they subconsciously resent it. If, however, they are aware of the reluctance they can easily overcome it.

As I have said, medium-sexed men and women present by far the largest proportion of the human race. It is for them that I am writing this book, so I shall say nothing more about the highly-sexed – they are well equipped to look after themselves – nor shall I say anything about the lowly-sexed, for they require very special consideration which, I think, would be out of place here.

We have, then, reached the point when there is only one other aspect of love-making which has to be considered before we discuss the technique of love-play – the positions for making love.

6. Positions

It is quite surprising how prevalent is the notion that there is only one position, or maybe two, which human males and females can assume for intercourse – the insertion of the penis into the vagina.

As a teenager, some time before the last war, I was sent to Paris to study at the Sorbonne. Among the more precocious of us there was somewhat secretively circulated a little manual which had the title *The Thirty-Two Positions of Love*. The Hindus, too, have the guidance of a sexual-religious handbook which describes between three and four dozen 'attitudes for love'. The illustrations of both books, however, showed quite clearly that while one would have to be extremely athletic to be able to contort the limbs for some of the positions – indeed one or two would tax the advanced student of Yoga – there are half a dozen or so which are not only within every able-bodied man's and woman's capabilities to adopt, but whose use is an excellent and essential preventive of that enemy of sex activity – as of all other activity – boredom, about which I shall say more presently.

First, let us consider the so-called 'natural' position, the one supposed, as I have just said, to be the only one human beings can assume.

Most sex-education books call it the face-to-face-man-above position, the ease with which it can be assumed is much in its favour.

Penetration for the average Englishman denotes the final stage of the intercourse. Your partner, however, unlike many of his experienced brothers of other countries and cultures, proceeds rapidly towards orgasm once he has inserted his penis, whereas insertion can be used as an intermediate stage; that is, it can be a technique for the gradual heightening of sensation instead of merely the vehicle for natural climax.

The man who regards penetration as the final stage brings his lover and himself to the brink of the point-of-no-return before inserting his penis. For this reason it is essential that the method of coupling he employs should be easy to assume. If he were to adopt a position which required some bodily adjustment before he and his partner were one hundred per cent comfortable – which is an essential of any position if the intensity of the orgasm is not to be adversely affected – the necessity to handle the penis, or to insert and withdraw it once or twice before it was properly in position in the vagina, would most probably bring him off while his partner still had some way to go.

To assume the face-to-face position takes the minimum of movement on the part of both, and probably a maximum of five seconds' time. The woman is already on her back – a position which she took up at the very first approach of her partner and probably did not alter throughout the whole period of preliminary love-play – and she has only to part her legs so that her partner may place his own legs between hers and his torso above hers.

If the tone of what I have written seems to imply that I have not a very good opinion of this position, it is only because I want to try to break through the kind of barrier which seems to block the imagination of so many ordinarily intelligent men and women.

This position has a good deal to recommend it, besides the ease with which it can be adopted. Sight, if the couple do not confine their love-making to complete darkness, is quite a powerful arousal factor. Sexual sensations that are at all strong invariably reveal the pleasurable effects they are having in the facial expressions of the partner. The face-to-face position is extremely well suited to allow the man and woman to look at each other, and the pleasure which the one is enjoying when seen cannot fail to have a heightening effect on the sensations of the other.

Or again, mouth-to-mouth kisses, particularly for the woman, have the effect of rousing the sensations strongly. I am not referring to the mouth-to-mouth kiss in which the lips merely touch one another, but the kind known as the 'deep kiss', in which the tongue explores the partner's mouth, or the lower lip, or tongue, is sucked by the other partner. A kiss of this kind at the moment of orgasm can add greatly to the intensity of the orgasmic sensations. Kisses upon other parts of the head and throat are almost equally rousing – as I shall be explaining shortly – and such kisses, of course, are easily executed in this position.

Another advantage is the ease with which the man can control the movements of his penis, which gives him a greater facility in timing his progress towards orgasm. But this advantage is effective only because, from the position she is in, the woman can make only cursory movements. In addition, it is possible for the man, by taking his own weight on his knees and one elbow, to free the other hand for fondling one or other of the woman's nipples. However, except for kissing, these advantages are not peculiar to this position; as we shall see, in some of the other positions they occur even more effectively.

Of the disadvantages – which again are not extreme – the first is that in this position penetration cannot be very deep, even under the most favourable physical circumstances; and here I must explain what I mean by physical circumstances.

The positioning of the entrance to the vagina is not exactly the same in each woman, but varies from individual to individual. The variation is not great, a maximum of merely two or three centimetres, but it is surprising the difference in accessibility to penetration the forward or backward setting of the vaginal entrance can make to the depth of penetration.

The forward-setting is the more advantageous, but even with a penis of average length it allows penetration to little more than half the vaginal length. The backward-setting not only lessens his depth of penetration, but it can, if set well back, cause the man some discomfort by requiring the penis to adopt an unnatural angle to achieve penetration at all.

Nor is it the actual positioning of the vaginal entrance alone which produces these circumstances. The advantage of a forward-set entrance can be almost completely nullified by the slimness of the buttocks; while, conversely, the disadvantageous feature of a backward-set entrance can be corrected by buttocks of prominent contours.

A little experimentation will soon disclose whether the natural setting – either with or without the aid of the buttocks – is allowing the deepest possible penetration. It should be remembered that it is the entrance which is most thrown upwards that makes this possible; and where the physique does not naturally do this, correction can easily be made by placing a pillow, or even pillows, under the woman's buttocks, thus lifting her pubic area up towards the man's pubic area.

You will probably be wondering why I have seemed to be advocating deep penetration here, when I have said in Chapter 2 that the achievement of the most intense orgasm is as possible with an average-length or below-average-length penis as with one of above average length; and when I have repeatedly said that the vaginal nerves are not capable, except in comparatively rare cases, of producing orgasm on their own. The fact is that most women as they approach the point-of-no-return, and thereafter until orgasm has begun to subside, experience a strong need for deep penetration. At this point the woman will strain against the man, clearly trying to push the penis ever deeper into her. The man very often experiences a similar need, which he may actually express in whispered words to his partner as he tries to effect deeper penetration. The need in both is almost completely psychological in origin. The woman has a conscious, or often a subconscious, notion that the deeper the man's penis goes into her the more completely does she become physically fused with him; and physical fusion is an expression of the mental demand for the entire possession which every woman believes she must have of the father of her children. He must belong to her and only to her, and for this reason she is prepared to give herself utterly to him, as a means of binding him to her; and physical fusion symbolizes this for her.

It should not be thought that the need to fulfil these ambitions is present at every intercourse. Much depends on the mood of the man or woman; the need may spring from a sudden thought, a sudden desire. But when it occurs it comes at a fairly late stage in the progress towards orgasm, more often than not when the husband has come to the point-of-no-return, and then it is too late for any adjustments to be made to allow for deeper penetration than is already achieved. For this reason, both partners should always be prepared, by assuring that the deepest penetration that the position adopted will allow is made possible from the very first moment of coupling, for the deepest physical penetration will do much to achieve psychological satisfaction.

In the face-to-face-man-above position this means taking those mechanical measures – the placing of pillows under the buttocks of the woman or any other means which the couple have discovered – which will raise her pubic area to the height that experimentation has shown to be necessary to allow the penis to reach the furtherest possible recesses of the vagina when the woman is lying with her legs stretched straight. If this is done, should she feel the need, or should her partner indicate that he feels the need of deep penetration at a time too late to make positional adjustments, she can easily and quickly increase the depth of penetration to the maximum this position allows by drawing up her knees towards her breasts as far as they will go without discomfort. If she then crosses the lower part of her legs over the small of her partner's back, exerting a downward pressure with them on his back, and can, at the same time, firmly press her hands, one on each of her partner's buttocks, even though the actual physical penetration may not be very much deeper, there is a sensation in both partners that very deep penetration is being achieved.

*   *   *

The second position is a variation of the one just described. Its name – face-to-face-woman-above – explains the principle of it. The man lies on her back, his legs together, and the woman crouches over him, her legs drawn up on either side of his thighs, her torso bent over and almost touching his. The penis is then inserted, either by the woman or by the man and the woman then stretches out first one leg, then the other, and lowers herself upon her partner.

This position has these advantages. It allows sight of the partner, deep kissing and other kissing; it leaves both the man's hands free to caress both nipples simultaneously and to stroke other erotically sensitive parts of her back and outer thighs; and it permits the woman, in fact requires her, to make the main movements, and so make it possible for her to regulate her own approach to orgasm.

This latter, however, can be a disadvantage to the man, if he cannot control his own *faster* rhythm. On the other hand, if he does come before his partner she can continue to make the necessary movements until she has reached orgasm herself. If this situation occurred while the couple were in the first position, it would be necessary for the husband to continue his movements, and to do so after orgasm has been reached gives him some discomfort, for he is denied the natural relief of total relaxation of body and mind which is the inescapable result of intense orgasmic sensation. With the woman making the movements the man is able to relax.

Perhaps the most important advantage of this second position is derived when, despite the fact that he is physically weary, the man has an intense desire for orgasm. His weariness will almost certainly prevent his erection from being a strong one, and if this has happened, though his penis will be stiff enough to allow the orgasm-producing nerves to function to climax – in the fully relaxed penis they are not able to do this – it may be so comparatively limp that it would slip out if the man were in the above-position. Alternatively, the limp penis requires much longer stimulation to achieve orgasm, and the movements the man makes can quickly tire him if he is already generally weary. The first disadvantage can be overcome if the man opens his legs once the penis has been inserted, and the woman closes hers and places them between the man's which has the effect of allowing the vagina to grip the penis. This, however, reduces penetration considerably.

*   *   *

A third face-to-face position is that in which the partners lie on their sides, turned to one another. Many sex-counsellors advocate this position, because it is not so physically tiring as either of the two other positions just described. Personally, however, I find the disadvantages attaching to it disproportionate to the benefit derived.

First of all, it requires a certain degree of physical ingenuity to achieve, even if penetration is effected in the face-to-face-man-above position and the couple then slowly turn over on to their sides, making sure that the penis remains in the vagina while they are doing so. If the attempt is made to effect penetration from the side position, even if the couple know what to do, they will nearly always experience some awkwardness in making connection.

Let us suppose that the man is lying on his right side. The woman will raise her left (lower) leg and pass it over the man's right leg, bending it slightly at the knee and pushing the thigh high up between his legs. The man will then pass his left leg over, at the same time manoeuvring the penis into position– it will be found that the woman must nearly always assist him by drawing the outer and inner lips apart– and when connection is made he will thrust this leg over as far as it will go. The woman will then pass her right leg over her partner's left leg, bending it so that, if possible, she can take a purchase on her partner's left thigh-bone with the crook of her leg.

Connection in this position can only be made at all if the vaginal entrance is set well forward. If it is set back, it may just be possible for the head of the penis only to enter. No physical adjustment can be made to correct the natural setting of the vaginal entrance.

Earlier on I pointed out that the nerves of the vaginal entrance are particularly sensitive to the entry and withdrawal of the penis, producing sensations unlike any other, which are certainly conducive to orgasm. Many couples will find that if they can be patient enough to adopt the side-by-side position at all and aim at no more than introducing little of the penis besides the head, these particular sensations are experienced as in no other position, and their occasional promotion can bring a welcome novelty to intercourse. It has been found by some who have occasionally used this position for this purpose that very often the experience has been spoiled for them by the slippery penis losing contact with the vagina at the moment of the man's orgasm. Warning should be taken from this, and steps taken to see that it is avoided.

The chief objection of this position, as I see it, is that even with a perfectly physically matched couple the fullest penetration that it is possible to achieve can never be more than half, and nothing that the couple can do can improve on this should the need for the sensation of deep penetration come on them after the point-of-no-return has been reached.

*   *   *

Undoubtedly the most satisfactory of the recumbent positions from the point of view of deep penetration and the freedom it allows to both partners to indulge in caresses is what is known as the woman-astride position.

The man lies on his back, his legs together. The woman then squats astride him, her knees drawn up to her breasts and, the penis having been inserted, she lowers herself right down until she is sitting firmly upon his upper hips, the lower part of her pubic area resting upon his lower body.

Penetration is now the deepest that can possibly be achieved in any position. You will recall that when I was referring to the sensitivity of the vagina I said that the very far end of the vagina which cannot normally be reached by an average-length penis, or even by some of the above average length, does produce very intense erotic sensations, but appears to be only capable of this if it is stretched. In this position penetration is so deep that this type of stretching does take place. This is the only position in which the penis – which, in any case, provides the only means to perform this stretching – can penetrate to the requisite depth to do so.

In order to experience these sensations the woman must sit upright. If she bends her body forward more than twenty or thirty degrees the sensations almost cease, but are restored as soon as she sits upright again. By brief, very simple experiments she will quickly discover that if she sits up and maintains the sensations it will not be long before they develop into an exquisite experience with makes her actually catch her breath and cry out with pleasure. If the sensations become too much for her to bear, and she must have relief, she leans forward. When the intensity has retreated, if she returns to the upright position, the sensations return; and each time the process is repeated the more the intensity increases, so that without making any other movements but sitting back and leaning forward she can bring herself off.

If, at the same time, her partner is stimulating a nipple and the clitoris with his fingers, the different quality of the sensations these organs produce combined with the others bring about the most intense orgasm a woman can experience. Even those with a medium sex-urge can be so overcome that for a couple of seconds they may lose consciousness.

The only activity possible in the face-to-face positions which is not possible here is kissing; but this is more than compensated for by the other sensations, in which the man, while not experiencing the same type of sensations as the woman, nevertheless achieves the most intense sensations peculiar to him, while, in any case, the sensitive lover is proportionately affected by the satisfaction his partner is achieving.

The effect of his partner sitting firmly on his upper thighs is to stretch the skin covering the body of the penis. This stretching pulls on the strand of ordinary skin which is joined to the head of the penis on the underside just at the point where the orgasm-producing nerves are, and produces a sensation which never occurs when they are stimulated in any other way. Immediately the pulling is applied the sensation begins, and increases with a much slower tempo than the sensations produced by other forms of stimulation. This particular sensation is much more widely diffused than the pre-orgasmic sensations, being felt from the moment it begins, in the inside of the thighs from the scrotum to half-way to the knees, and right inside the lower part of the belly, from where, in particularly sensitive men, it jumps to the nipples. If the woman is able to reach the man's nipples without leaning forward, she can increase the area of sensation to practically the whole of the body by gently caressing the nipples with her fingers.

If the pulling is exerted with a constant pressure for long enough the man will come without either he or his partner having to make any movements. Each time the woman leans forward to relieve her own sensations she relaxes the pulling pressure on the penis, and the man's sensations subside. But the moment she returns to the upright the sensations of both begin again, each time with increased intensity. If the man's nipples are fondled, the sensation this produces, added to the visual and audible stimuli of the woman's own ecstasy, so affect the man that he too experiences an intensity of orgasm such as he achieves from no other position.

I do not recommend frequent use of this position. Rather it should be saved for those occasions when the couple are under the influence of a particularly strong emotional urge to demonstrate their mutual love. I say this because the climax achieved – if the position is correctly assumed, and the actions are properly executed – can be such an experience that it should be savoured, kept in reserve for very special occasions, free from the risk of becoming jaded.

It is surprising how many couples there are to whom it has not occurred that it is not necessary to have a bed to lie on for love-making, nor to take up a recumbent position for the successful conclusion of intercourse.

A variation of the last position can be made if the man can lie with his back supported by the bed, and his buttocks by a stool or some such narrow thing the same height as the bed – say a blanket-chest. The woman takes up a position standing with her legs astraddle the blanket chest, or whatever is being used, and she then lowers herself on to her partner until the penis is inserted and she is sitting firmly on him as before, but keeping her feet on the ground. Penetration is still deeper than can be achieved in any other position except one, which I shall shortly describe, but not deep enough to produce the stretching sensations in her, nor the pulling sensations in her partner.

Because there are no bed-clothes to hinder movement and because her feet have something to press against, thus making it possible for her to carry out movements that are wider in scope than she could make in the previous position, she can induce in herself and in her partner pre-orgasmic and orgasmic sensations of the more common variety. They will, however, be much more intense. Also, as she is more firmly balanced she can can be much more active with her hands in caressing and fondling her partner and he can apply stimulation to her inner thighs, as well as to her breasts and clitoris, of a much more determined nature than he felt it wise to do when she was more precariously balanced, and she is in any case completely in control of his and her own sensations. The effect, too, of air circulating round the naked bodies of both, and of the sight of much more of each other's bodies than most other positions permit, is to produce additional stimuli, which increase the intensity of the immediate pre-climax and the climax experiences.

This position – can, I suppose, be classified as semi-recumbent, and there is a variation on it which many couples occasionally find convenient. A low bed is essential for its execution. The woman assumes the position which the man assumed in the last position – that is, she lies on the bed, with her buttocks on or slightly over the edge; however, instead of stretching out her legs on a stool or blanket-chest as the man did, she bends them at the knees so that her feet are firmly on the floor. The man then kneels between her legs and inserts his penis. (If the bed is too high for him to do this by kneeling on the floor, he must make adjustments of some kind which will bring his pubic area on a level with hers). Penetration is quite deep, but only so long as the woman lies flat on her back and does not raise her feet from the floor; the man's hands are left free to stimulate clitoris and breast, or any other sensitive area of the body presented to him; but it does preclude kissing, and the woman can do nothing to stimulate the man with her hands. Some couples, however, find it most satisfactory for occasional use.

✻   ✻   ✻

The next position is known as the face-to-face-seated. Here
the man sits on an ordinary chair and the woman sits astride
him. This position allows reasonably deep penetration, but
there are other advantages which no other position permits. If
the woman, having placed her hands on the man's shoulders,
leans very slightly back, he is able to caress her breasts with his
mouth; all the most erotically sensitive areas, particularly of
the back, are within reach of light stimulation of his hands;
while the clitoris is easily accessible to the stimulation of his
fingers. Couples with a tendency to corpulence claim to find
this position most helpful in obtaining for them comparatively
deep penetration; but the normally built couple will probably
find that the greatest disadvantage for them is that it does not
permit satisfaction of the late need for deeper penetration.

*   *   *

Many young couples, who have been unfortunate enough not
to find a house or even a room they can share, either in the
home of one or the other's parents or anywhere else, are often
hard put to it to find opportunities or suitable conditions in
which they may express their love for one another in love-
making intercourse. Much more frequently than the more
fortunate imagine, these young people must often make love
furtively, with little or no time for love-play and in situations
where only the face-to-face-standing position is feasible.

   This position can only be successfully taken without adjustments of any kind when the couple are more or less of the
same height. If the woman is shorter than the man, she must
stand on something to raise her pubic area to a level with his;
but even if this is accomplished, much will depend on the
setting of the vaginal entrance, which ought to be forward in
order for there to be a chance of reasonably deep penetration
being effected. Since the conditions under which the couple
are making love require them to be fully clothed, there is no
chance of additional stimulation except deep kissing. Nevertheless, couples so unhappily situated should not spurn this
position, for it does at least allow them to give themselves to
one another and it can be emotionally satisfying even if the

physical results leave much to be desired.

There is a variation of the face-to-face-standing position which I feel I must mention in order to condemn it. It is called by some of its advocates 'The Tree', and it has somehow penetrated our sex-awareness after a longish journey from the Orient.

The man stands, his feet apart to give him a firm posture, and his partner stands facing him, with her feet apart also. The penis is inserted, and the woman clasps his hands under her buttocks. At a pre-arranged signal the man lifts the woman's buttocks at the same time that she swings both her feet off the ground, grips the man's hips between her thighs, and, if posible, crosses her feet in the small of his back. The position gives the sensation of reasonably deep penetration.

The dangers of it are, of course, immediately apparent. If for some reason the man's support of the woman's body on his hands is removed, the whole weight of her body is taken by the penis, however much she may grip his hips with her thighs. For the man this, though lasting only a few seconds before recovery is made, may strain the root of the penis – that part which lies within his body – causing internal lacerations in some cases, and in every case great pain. For the woman the results can be much more serious, particularly if the penis is of above-average length. Since erection is bound to be strong, the penis cannot slip out of the vagina easily from this position. As the weight of the woman forces it downwards into an unnatural alignment parallel with the floor, it resists, with the result that it can tear the interior of the vagina and sometimes the lower part of the entrance. But whether this happens or not, there will inevitably be great pain.

There is also the risk of something of this sort happening while penetration is being effected. The penis must be inserted before the woman takes up her position astraddle her partner's hips. If the man is taller than the woman he will have to bend his knees to bring his pubic area level with his partner's that that the penis may enter her. Bending the knees reduces the stability of his equilibrium – unless he is quite strong – and in attempting to preserve his balance he may involuntarily move his pubic area in such a way that the penis may damage the entrance to the vagina; while a similar risk is run if the man tries to straighten his knees before the woman has taken up her position astraddle his hips.

I could go on pointing out further risks of great pain and possible damage, but I think I have said enough to make it quite clear that 'The Tree' is a dangerous position to adopt. Apart from the potential danger, however, the position has little to commend it, for there can be no subsidiary stimulation beyond deep kissing.

*   *   *

The final position I wish to describe here has as much in its favour as 'The Tree' has against it, and yet, curiously enough, among English people it is practised probably with the least frequency of any position. With other peoples, however, it is one of the favourite positions, particularly among the French, after whom it is sometimes called the French position, though we refer to it simply as the rear-entry position, or rear position.

The woman kneels on the bed on her hands and knees, with her legs apart. The man kneels behind her and inserts his penis from that position. Adjustments can quite easily be made to allow for the different heights of man and woman. In every case penetration is exceptionally deep, but where the vaginal entrance is set back the depth of penetration almost equals that experienced in the face-to-face-woman-astride position. If, in addition, the man's penis is slightly above average length, the woman will also experience the 'stretching' sensations of the astride position, though the man will not have the 'pulling' sensations.

While mouth-to-mouth kissing is not possible, and the partner's face cannot be seen, the man's hands are left free for stimulation of the nipples and clitoris, while he is also able to administer light kisses to the erotically sensitive areas of the woman's back, and the movements of his lower belly will also stimulate the very sensitive area at the base of the woman's spine.

Altogether, this position has much to commend it. Most of the prejudice against it is in the woman's mind, and is a legacy of her Victorian experience of and approach to sex. This is the position which nearly all animals adopt for copulation, and she has the idea that it is, therefore, degrading for her to allow connection to be made in this way. A sensitive woman, however, is usually also an intelligent one, as she might with profit tell herself that, the very fact that humans are able to adopt any number of positions demonstrates that sex superiority over the animal world; and the assumption of the rear-entry position adds to, rather than detracts from, that superiority.

Here, then, are the positions which men and women can assume without difficulty. As experience increases, other variations will most likely occur to both; and if they do neither partner should hesitate to experiment. Such experiments keep alive the freshness of practical sex, in which, though you might not believe it could be possible, 'the same old routine' can be as boring and as great an enemy to sustained delight in sex as it can be soul-destroying an any other aspect of our daily lives.

We now have all the knowledge we require to allow us to consider what is undoubtedly as important to successful intercourse as the technique of penetration. I like to call it practical love-making, though it is variously known as love-play, or fore-play – the preparation of both man and woman, and particularly the latter, for the achievement of orgasm. Since love-play precedes penetration, you are probably thinking it is a bit odd of me to have talked about positions before the technique of love-play. The fact is that during our consideration of love-play it will be essential to refer, from time to time, to one or other of the positions. By describing the positions first we shall not have to digress in order to explain what is meant by, or the sensations that can be achieved by, this or that position.

7. Practical Love-making

You probably know from experience, but I shall refer to it for convenience's sake, that light touches with the hand, lips or tip of the tongue practically anywhere on your body have the effect of stimulating you sexually. There are, however, certain areas of the skin that are much more sensitive than others; they are called *erogenous zones*.

Among the most sensitive of your erogenous zones are your lips, behind your ears, the nape of your neck, your throat, your armpits, your breasts, your stomach – particularly your navel; the outer and inner vaginal lips, the inside of the thighs, somewhat curiously the back of the knees, and the whole length of the spine – especially the base. Your partner's caresses in any of these regions cannot fail to give you physical pleasure and equally cannot fail to intensify your erotic sensations.

Your partner is not quite so well-equipped with erogenous zones. His mouth is a little less sensitive than yours, but does respond to sucking and very mild biting. His throat, behind the ears, and the nape of his neck are about as sensitive as yours are. As I have already pointed out, some men derive stimulation from caresses of the nipples with the fingers and lips. Your partner's navel is certainly sensitive and the base of his spine is more sensitive than yours, while his buttocks respond to both light and quite heavy pressure with differing results. But, like you, the whole area of his skin is sensitive to a greater or lesser degree.

Caresses in the erogenous zones play a considerable role in love-play, as can be imagined, but much of the effect of them can be lost if any sort of covering intervenes, even a flimsy nightdress or an open pyjama jacket. Many couples, these days, sleep naked as a regular practice; but even if you do not, I strongly advise that as soon as either of you indicate a desire for intercourse whatever you are wearing should be removed. During love-play it will not only be fingers and lips which will be in contact with each other's bodies: the limbs of one partner will be constantly brushing against the limbs of the other, and this quite casual contact of naked flesh with naked flesh provides a further stimulant.

In addition, whatever position you assume for coupling, the bodies must touch, and again the contact of naked flesh with naked flesh adds considerably to the total effect. The difference between making love with only the briefest covering and in complete nakedness can be likened to the difference between swimming in a costume, even the briefest of bikinis, and swimming nude.

The only reason for a couple not making love naked is that some shyness still persists. In the early days of partnership if there were any shyness it was natural, but I hope that both of you have outgrown it. If you have not, every effort should be made to eliminate it. You should remember that between lovers nothing is private – not even the so-called private parts.

If clothes can be tiresome, jewellery can be a menace. Never make love without first removing all rings, bracelets, necklaces and earrings. Rings can be quite dangerous, for it is very easy to scratch your partner painfully if you make a sudden movement with your hands at any time during love-play.

Attention to the cleanliness of the sexual parts is also of the greatest importance. If you do not bath every day, the washing of the sex organs should become a part of your cleansing routine on rising and before you go to bed.

Partly because of lack of opportunity at other times of the day – through absence of one or both partners from the home, or the presence of a young family needing attention, or merely lack of time – the majority of couples leave their love-making until they go to bed at night. It is a great pity that our organization for living practically forces this on us, because neither of us is really at our best after a hard day's work.

But the sexual urge does not – as probably all of us know – confine itself to the late hours; and desire recognizes no clock. So it follows that love-making is not solely a nocturnal activity. I am strongly of the view that if one of the couple wishes to make love at any time of the day and circumstances are favourable, the other should respond. We should sieze every opportunity to break away from the time-rut into which the way we have organized our lives has thrust us. We should make the most of weekends, casual holidays and the longer vacations to show one another that we are loving each other all the time.

I have already hinted, too, that the bedroom and the bed are not essential adjuncts of love-making. Supposing the woman becomes aware of rising sexual tension while she and her partner are, say, in the sitting-room in the mid-evening, what is to prevent her from slipping away to make herself ready and returning in a couple of minutes, whispering to her partner, 'I want to be loved'? The very act of helping one another to undress is, by its novelty, a stimulant, and the use of cushions on the floor, or the settee, or an armchair, and finally one of the positions for which the bed is not suitable, make the experience a memorable one; for the unusualness and slight daring of it, and the unexpectedness and spontaneity of the woman's desire, and her appeal to her partner to love her, will inevitably endow the climax with a long-remembered intensity.

If you have been living a couple of years or so with a partner ignorant of his own and your sexual potentialities, or at best sexually unimaginative, I do not think you will have to be told how easily the practice of sex can fall into a routine which will lead to a boredom which, in turn, can threaten the whole relationship.

I once heard of the case of a young woman, Jenny. She had been married for three years, and she had been unfaithful to her husband; she was sorry, yet at the same time glad; she had no remorse and yet she had doubts; she loved him still, yet she was disappointed in him. This is how she described what had happened.

'David [her husband] and I are pretty well matched sexually. He is kind and considerate, and since our wedding night we have never made love without my having an orgasm, and we make love three or four times a week. I like making love, but the last year or so it has stopped being a joy.

'Do you know the play *A Quiet Weekend*, where the wife is nearly driven potty by her husband's habits? She knows that when he comes down to breakfast he'll say exactly what he said yesterday morning and the morning before that and before that?

'Well, it's like that with me and David's love-making. As soon as he puts out his hand and passes it over my body and my thighs, I know that he'll come back to my left breast, fondle the nipple for half a minute with his fingers, then he'll lean over me and run his lips and the tip of his tongue on my throat, suck the lobe of my right ear for three or four seconds, come down over my shoulder and right breast, and caress the nipple with his lips, and so on – and so on – and so on!

'I know every single move he's going to make and the order in which he will make them, and though I haven't the strength, or rather the control, to resist what he does, and we never fail to come practically together, I could scream every time he comes to me. If only he would do something different! If only he could give me some new sensation, even if it was just a little one.

'Well, we were asked to a party a week or two ago, and at the last moment he had to go away for his firm, but I went on my own. It wasn't a debauch, but it was a merry party, and among the merrier was Peter. I don't quite know how it happened, but I suddenly woke up to the fact that I was in a dark passage leading to our hostess's kitchen and Peter was kissing me. It was the first time that a man had kissed me since I'd married David, and I didn't care for it much. Then he touched me. I have never been touched like that before, and I almost came in a minute or so.

'Peter certainly knew what he was doing. He read me like a

book. When he suggested we slipped away to his flat, I knew what he meant, and I said yes eagerly. What had happened had made me realize what I suppose had been eating me up for months, that I wanted to be made love to by someone who didn't do what David did: or if they did, not as any kind of routine, but would keep me guessing.

'Well, it worked. It isn't a question of my stopping loving David, or of my loving Peter. It's a question of how I can make David make love to me like Peter does. You see, every time David comes to me now I try to stop myself wanting to shriek by attempting to imagine it's Peter who's with me. But it doesn't work, because David doesn't make love like Peter does.'

At the beginning I said, at some length, that the woman must be in equal partnership with the man in their sex relationship and that she could achieve this by taking the initiative herself, and conducting the intercourse from the first love-play to orgasm. Jenny's reaction to David's routine was only one reaction. She wanted to scream at the unvarying love-play habits which David had acquired, and she wanted to do so because, being fairly highly sexed, she reached orgasm as a result of what he did, despite the unchanging course of every coitus. But supposing she had been less highly sexed. Instead of wanting to scream, she might have become so bored, that the sameness of David's routine would have made her apathetic and she might have lost the facility for reaching orgasm altogether. From then on, neuroses would have developed and the whole relationship would have begun to crumble.

Further investigation showed that David was quite ignorant of at least six of the positions I have described in the last chapter, and of much that I shall write in this. As he saw it, his responsibility towards Jenny in their sex-relationship was to see that she always came. He had discovered a series of caresses to which she never failed to respond. As a result of what he did she always achieved orgasm, and it would have been stupid in his opinion, having discovered an effective formula, to have 'monkeyed around', as he put it, 'doing something else which in the end might not have brought her off'.

*   *   *

The fact that we nearly always make love in bed at night of itself almost inevitably envelopes us in a routine; and unless both partners are aware of the danger routine represents to their sex-lives, within practically no time at all a dreariness will inevitably colour their love-making, and though physically they may be satisfied, mentally they will become insensitive with frustration.

A young Frenchman once said to me a long time ago, 'The Englishman, usually practical to the point of coldblooded-ness, amazes me by his ignorance of the practice of sex. Making love should be as mentally exciting as it is physically exhilarating; it should be treated like a fine wine, sipped slowly, rolled round the tongue and savoured; it should be a promoter of joy, of smiles and laughter, and above all love. But your Englishmen gulps it down like he does his horrible strong beer. Three thrusts of his buttocks and it's all over.'

Like most, if not all, generalizations, this one did not do justice to many Englishmen, but it did describe graphically the attitude of very large numbers, who treat love-making with a perfunctoriness which, though orgasm for both is achieved, makes the whole operation spiritless, and eventually as boring as the routine.

Quite honestly, men and women must be bold and adventurous in their sexual approaches to one another if they are to derive the greatest benefits physically and psychologically from love-making, if they are to become fully developed, rounded persons and personalities. There is no end to the variety of love, and all that is required is a realization that a routine of caressing can be as sickening as an unchanging diet of roast beef. There is no reason at all why love-making should not be as exciting after thirty years as it was after thirty days. But it will not be unless both man and woman are constantly exploring themselves and each other.

It is to breach the routine-element of love-making in bed at night that I have said make love during the day, in the bedroom though not necessarily on the bed, in the sitting-room or any other room, whenever desire prompts and circumstances make it possible. If it happens only once or twice a year it is worth it; so seize the opportunity whenever you can.

But variation of time and place is only one of the lesser weapons in your armoury against the boredom of familiarity. As I have already said, probably more than once, there is no end to the variety of love-making. But the variety lies not so much in the discovery of new sensations as in the technique by which you excite the sensations you already know yourself capable of experiencing; and logically it follows that if both partners play an active role the possibilities of technical variations are doubled.

Now, perhaps, it will at last become clear to you why I have said from the very first pages of this book that the woman must be an equal partner, that she must be granted as much right to be active as custom has granted to the man. To help you towards this end, I have described the potentialities of your partner's and our own sexual apparatus, and how each reacts to certain stimuli. Now I want to further this education by indicating to you how the stimuli can be applied to bring the desired and desirable ends – note the plural – to your love-making.

It is most important, however, that you should remember from this point onwards that I am NOT setting out a routine of love-making. I am not going to say, 'Do this and then this, in this order, and then go on to this'; but I am going to try to show you what the effect of doing certain things will be, and then leave you to work out for yourself how and in what order, in what combinations and variations, you can apply them to your partner and to yourself.

In the course of what I shall be saying I am going to explode one or two fairly widely held fallacies.

The first is that a woman cannot rouse herself sexually to the point at which orgasm is possible shortly after coupling, without the concentrated attentions of her partner. (This, of course, excludes self-stimulation of the clitoris, which is the most common form of female self-relief.) To make absolutely clear what I mean by this, let me go into a little more detail.

The man, as we know, can achieve orgasm within one or two minutes of inserting his penis in the vagina at the moment he has reached full erection, and without any previous stimulation.

We know, too, that even when the woman is strongly aroused several minutes of clitoral stimulation are required to bring her off; and, further, that, unless she is one of a very small company who are peculiar in this respect, vaginal stimulation alone cannot bring her to orgasm.

Because of these *facts* a notion is extremely widely held that the woman is so difficult to bring off that a long period of physical stimulation is absolutely necessary to achieve this end.

It is surprising, but nevertheless a fact that very many seem to forget, that the very act of stimulating the partner is in itself stimulating. The experience of this man, who was seeking advice on how to slow down the tempo of his own arousal, is a quite common experience: 'I wondered if it might help if I began caressing my wife before I had an erection; but within ten seconds of putting my hand between her thighs or taking her nipple between my lips I have a full erection and the sensation that orgasm is not far off.'

I am sure you will be able to bear me out that this is true of the woman from your own experience. You are being caressed by your partner, lying quite passively while your own sensations are steadily mounting. Then quite suddenly you feel your partner's penis brush against you, and with the quality of being startled you experience an immediate upward leap in the intensity of your sensations. Or you put out your hand to caress your partner's penis, and the same thing happens. With this experience, it is surely nonsense to say that the woman can be aroused only by stimulation of one of her erogenous zones; insistence that she must be so stimulated is one of the arguments put forward for not allowing her to be the active partner.

The stimulation of oneself through the act of stimulating the partner is very largely psychological in origin; and this psychological stimulation can be increased until it produces a very high state of physical arousal purely by concentrating the thoughts on your erotic desires; for example, the anticipation of the orgasmic sensations, or even the encouragement of erotic images, which, like practically everything sexual a husband and wife can do, is not a sign of depravity in a married couple in the act of making love.

✳   ✳   ✳

Here I want to interpose a sentence or two concerning the agents of stimulation that are available to men and women, but first of all let me assure you that there is nothing depraved in what I am going to describe.

The obvious agents for both are the fingers and hands, the mouth and the tongue. In addition, the man has his penis; the woman her breasts.

The activities which the fingers and hands can perform are too evident to need describing, and the obvious activities for the mouth and the tongue are kissing on the mouth and any other erogenous zone – any other erogenous zone including the genitals.

Genital kissing of both sexes is widely practised by continental peoples and orientals, but among the English it is practised only by a comparative few who have been extra bold in their love-making and extra keen in demonstrating their love.

The uninitiated hesitate to use the genital kiss because they have the mistaken idea that it is not quite 'nice', and that in any case it can be physically unpleasant to the senses of taste and smell. A brief moment of actual experience will be sufficient to show how wrong the latter is, provided the pubic area is clean.

You will know from experience that as soon as both man and woman are sexually roused the vagina and the penis exude a flow of lubricating secretions. It is the fear that these secretions will taste or smell unpleasant that holds back the inexperienced from making the genital kiss. In fact, *neither of the secretions has any taste or smell whatever;* and as the mouth continuously produces saliva in more than usual quantities during sexual arousal, they are also undetectable to the touch of tongue or lips. If there is a faint odour about the genitals at all, it will be very faint, but rather than be repellent it will have a definite aphrodisiac effect; that is to say, it will add to the sensations of arousal.

Any exponent of the genital kiss will quickly reassure you that there is nothing unpleasant about performing it, and that, on the contrary, the touch of the clitoris, of the inner and outer lips, can produce a tension which no other form of stimulation anywhere else on the body will produce.

Apart from mouth-kissing and genital-kissing, the mouth and tongue should be used as agents for stimulating the other erogenous zones. The tip of the tongue making quick movements in the navel cavity will send ripples of sensation down through the genitals and thighs as far as behind the knees. The same movements of the tip of the tongue in the cavities behind the ears is also more than usually stimulating, while running the slightly parted lips, with the tongue protruding just a little way between them, down the length of the spine and up and down the surfaces of the inner thighs will produce similar extra pleasure.

Sucking by both of the nipples of the other, and sucking of the clitoris by the man and of the head of the penis by the woman are even more effective still, particularly the latter.

All these activities, while stimulating the partner to whom they are applied, also cause stimulation, though to a lesser degree, in the active partner. There are, however, activities in which mutual physical stimulation can be achieved – activities, moreover, which produce a very high degree of simultaneous tension in each.

If the woman places herself astride her partner in a kneeling position, she is able to perform two of these actions. First, let her bend forward over her partner so that her nipples can be lightly placed upon his; then if she takes her own nipples between the thumb and forefinger of each hand and brushes them gently against her partner's nipples there is simultaneous stimulation, quite sharp for the woman, and for the man in proportion to the degree of erotic sensitivity there is in his nipples.

Next, by raising her haunches to the right height, she can take her clitoris. Here again the simultaneous sensations are extremely strong. If the man has a particularly strong erection, raising the penis to the angle at which it can make contact with the clitoris can cause him slight pain. This can be avoided if the woman turns about and takes up the same position, kneeling astride her partner, with her back to his face. In this position the penis will have to be raised only a very short way to make contact with the clitoris.

Many women at times feel a very strong desire not only to kiss and suck the penis, but to caress it between the breasts. (These desires can be exceptionally strong, and if they are not humoured can cause feelings of mental irritation.) If the woman has the desire to caress the man's penis with her breasts, she will find the most satisfactory position for doing so by kneeling between her partner's legs lowering herself over his pubic area. With a hand to either breast she then strokes the sides of the penis with them.

This produces simultaneous sensations, but they will not be so strong as when, taking the nipple of one breast between forefinger and thumb, she strokes the underside of the head of the penis with it. This is exceptionally stimulating to the man, as is the stroking of the clitoris with the penis, and unless it is intended to bring him to orgasm, when the eruption of the semen on the woman's organs can bring her to orgasm also, she must stop immediately the man indicates that he is progressing too far.

The achievement of orgasm for both partners is the end to which all intercourse is directed. But this should not be the sole ambition.

If there is to be orgasm, the orgasmic sensations should be as intense as it is possible to induce them to be. Except among the most experienced lovers, it is not usually appreciated that the intensity of orgasm can be heightened if the threshold of the point-of-no-return is reached several times, and each time allowed to subside before going on to the climax. Sound judgment is required of just how far to go, but with practice it can be done. At such moments the couple must stop all activity; though if there has been simultaneous stimulation which has brought the man farther forward than the woman, he can continue to stimulate her, provided he does not use any method which has the effect of heightening his own sensations.

It is difficult for either partner to be able to judge by the reactions of the other exactly how near the point-of-no-return is. It is necessary, therefore, for you and your partner to devise some means of communicating this to one another. It can be either a word signal or a touch signal or a slight movement of drawing away out of reach of the stimulating agent; but it must be sufficiently unmistakable for the partner to recognize it immediately and to stop at once. Two seconds, even one, can make all the difference.

Your reaction to such a signal from your partner is absolutely vital. Again and again I have mentioned the fact that the man, once roused, can achieve orgasm in a fraction of the time that the woman can achieve hers. It follows, therefore, that your stimulation of him can bring him to the point-of-no-return again and again before you have once reached that point yourself.

✻   ✻   ✻

What, then, is to be done to bring more synchronization to your sensations?

It is possible, by practice, for your partner voluntarily to reduce the speed of his progress by mental control. I am not going to suggest that he should go so far as many orientals do and smoke and read a book while the woman conducts the love-play. But he can direct his thoughts from love-making and the erotic images which fill his mind when the body is sexually roused. It need be only for a few moments, but it will be sufficient to retard him considerably, and be quite an effective stop. If, at the same time, you encourage erotic thoughts and images, you will bring yourself effectively forward. This takes a little practice, but it is quite within the scope of every man and woman.

There is one other method which you can use to speed up your own tempo. You will have noticed that when orgasm is approaching your heart begins to beat faster and faster and you begin to breathe more rapidly. By deliberately breathing more quickly through parted lips, you can increase your pulse-rate, and if you are already sexually roused this will have the effect of heightening your sensations.

But what can probably help you most is for your partner to apply mild stimulation himself. When you have taken the iniative in love-making, he will lie quietly on his back throughout unless you wish to apply your caresses to the erogenous zones of his back, and he will let you do whatever you like to him. He can still do this and move no more than a hand or arm to stroke you, to fondle your nipples, and to stroke your clitoris with a finger. Doing this will leave you absolutely free to move as you please, stimulate him in any way you wish and maintain the iniative; but at the same time you will benefit from his stimulation of you.

One of the most effective positions in which you can obtain mutual stimulation is achieved if you place yourself above your partner, your head towards his feet, and your pubic area over his face. If you lower yourself a little he is able to apply genital kisses to you, while you can simultaneously do the same to him. At the same time he can also caress your nipples, or stroke your back, or the sensitive areas of your buttocks. A warning is necessary, however! Even among the most experienced, this method of mutual stimulation produces the most intense sensations in a shorter time than any other method.

When you have taken the initiative it is logical for you to choose the position. Unless you wish your partner to take over after the penis has been inserted, you will obviously choose a position in which you still have the greater control. The face-to-face-woman-above or the woman-astride positions are the natural ones. You can adopt the face-to-face-seated position, but this will necessitate a break in rhythm, as it will mean both of you moving from the bed to go to the chair. However, you may occasionally feel that such a long pause would not be detrimental.

Many couples have the idea that as soon as the penis is inserted stimulation of the erogenous zones can cease, except that the man may fondle one of the nipples with the fingers, that the woman may caress the erogenous zones of the man's back and buttocks if the position assumed allows this, or that both may participate in deep-kissing. We have seen, however, that it is the stimulation of the clitoris which best produces orgasm in the majority of women.

It is in connection with clitoral stimulation that I wish to reveal the second fallacy. Perhaps *fallacy* is not quite the right word to use here; I think the better phrase would be general *misconception*!

It is widely imagined that the face-to-face-man-above position is the most satisfactory because it allows stimulation of the clitoris by the penis as the man makes thrusting movements with his buttocks.

Ages ago, before human beings had developed as far physically as they have today, it is quite possible that penis-clitoris contact was possible in this position. In fact, because the most powerful orgasm-producing nerves are situated in the clitoris, the two organs were so situated that contact was possible. But the female body has so modified through the centuries that the clitoris has become smaller and the angle of the vagina so adapted to allow entry of the penis in the face-to-face positions that, except where the clitoris is more than ordinarily large and the vaginal entrance is unusually small, penis-clitoris contact is almost certain to be unachievable unless the man attempts to insert his penis specifically to achieve it; but if he does this the angle of the penis will be such that only the head can be inserted, while the sensations produced in the penis and in the vaginal entrance by the bending of the stiffened member to achieve contact will be merely painful to both partners. This factor is not pointed out often enough. Naturally there are some couples so built that they do achieve spontaneous clitoris-penis contact but in my experience the couples who do not obtain this spontaneous contact far out-number them. And it is important that this should be known, for there is strong reason for believing that ignorance of it is a prominent reason for many women not achieving orgasm even though their partners are otherwise quite often experienced lovers.

It will now probably strike you why it was that when I was describing the positions for coupling I put high among the advantages the accessibility of the clitoris for stimulation *after* the position had been assumed. Since so many women cannot achieve orgasm by vaginal stimulation alone, it is essential that clitoral stimulation should be continued until the moment of the woman's orgasm, in many cases if she is to come at all, or if she is to experience anything like intense orgasmic sensations.

This clitoral stimulation should be performed by your partner with a finger. He can place his hand between his own and your pubic area, *after* he has inserted his penis. It will entail his holding himself slightly away from you, by arching his buttocks, and this will inevitably mean that the penis will not be able to penetrate much farther than halfway. At the same time that he stimulates the clitoris with a finger he will be able to make penile movements within the vagina. As soon as you feel yourself on the threshold of orgasm, at a sign from you he can withdraw his hand, and if you thrust your pubic area hard against his, the penile movements will be sufficient to bring you off, particularly if your partner has transferred his hand to the stimulation of the nipple, and with a sense of urgency – which he will almost certainly feel, but which, if he does not, he should simulate – kisses your throat and behind the ear, or sucks the flesh of your shoulder in its most sensitive spot.[1] In addition to the sensations produced by clitoral stimulation, the fact that the penis is only inserted a comparatively short way will stimulate the sensitive entrance to the vagina with the head of the penis, which does not usually happen when normal penetration is achieved. This, of course, adds to the accumulation of sensations.

There is one combination of physical features which may make clitoral stimulation by the man after penetration slightly difficult. If the penis is much below average in length, or the hand rather large and the stomach somewhat corpulent, it may not be possible for more than the head of the penis to penetrate. (Only very rarely can the penis not penetrate at all.) This may mean that penile movements cannot be made without the penis slipping out each time a backwards movement of the buttocks is made. On the other hand, if only the very slightest movements are possible, the man's orgasm-producing nerves in the head of the penis are brought into contact with the particularly sensitive vaginal entrance nerves and the mutual sensations are extremely intense.

Should your partner not be able to place his hand in position except by painfully contorting his arm, or should the

[1] Sucking of the flesh of an erogenous zone is known as love-biting. It has one disadvantage – it produces a mark on the skin rather like a bruise.

penis be so short that it cannot reach the vaginal entrance at all with the hand in position, you should place your own hand there. Many women have an aversion to stimulating themselves manually anywhere on their bodies in the last stage of intercourse. This aversion is of purely psychological origins, however; there are no moral or aesthetic reasons why a woman should not do so, and I suggest that if such an aversion exists efforts should be made to overcome it.

It is because of the inaccessibility of the clitoris in both the face-to-face-full-length positions that I am inclined to favour one of the other positions for more frequent use, one of the face-to-face positions being adopted as a 'change', so to speak. However, preferences in this matter are individual.

                                 *   *   *

Some pages back I said that four of the senses played a full part in love-making. We have considered the effect on the erotic sensations of touch, sight and smell. The fourth sense brought into play is hearing.

Many men and women, even some time before the threshold of the point-of-no-return is reached, experience sensations so intense that they involuntarily make exclamations of appreciation, or give little cries, or whimper – the volume of sound they emit increasing as the intensity of the sensations mounts, until they come to the accompaniment of quite loud cries.

If you do not react involuntarily in this way, I think you will be surprised how very easily and naturally it will come to you if you deliberately try it. What I think may surprise you even more is the effect your own exclamations and cries will have in heightening your own sensations. It is as if, by making audible sounds of appreciation, you are releasing restrictive inhibitions that seem to have remained in your approach to love-making and intercourse; and I think that this is very probably what happens. But not only is making sounds self-stimulating, the effect of yours on your partner and of his on you is as effective as many a touch-stimulus.

If you add sound to your other activities and your partner responds in the same way while you are making love to him, you will be brought even nearer to the point-of-no-return on your own initiative. If you really let go with a loud cry or exclamation at the moment of orgasmic climax you will add many degrees to the intensity of the experience for both of you.

Each individual will discover what words or sounds most stimulate her and her partner. The only guide I will give is that the words or sounds should be of *appreciation for what the partner is making you feel*; that is, admiration for his or her technique for bringing you to orgasm.

It would take a book three or four times the length of this one to describe all the variations and permutations of love-play, but I think I have given you here a fairly good basis from which you can develop your own techniques. A man who had served as a British agent during the Second World War and had been captured and tortured and starved by the Gestapo once said to me: 'What has really fascinated me in all my experience is that there really seems to be no end to what the body can accept under the most varied conditions.' He was talking of the body's capacity for undergoing strenuous physical attacks upon it, and its reactions to those attacks; but what he said applies equally to its love-making capabilities. No two sexual experiences need be the same if only man and woman, having the basic knowledge that I have given here, will be bold and imaginative. Making love can be as fresh and glorious an experience at sixty-five as it was the first time you did it at twenty.

Though I have given you here quite a broad foundation to work on, there still remain one or two points which frequently puzzle people, and on which I would like to offer guidance.

First, I have referred to the lubricating secretions which the penis exudes when a high state of sexual arousal has been brought about. As with practically everything else connected with the human body, the glands which produce these secretions do not work the same with everybody. In some men there is a most copious flow of this slippery, transparent and tasteless liquid from the penis within a few seconds of full erection; in others it may not appear until the threshold of the point-of-no-return is reached, and then may be only a few drops; in a few it may not appear at all – and this is nothing to worry about either.

Despite the fact that the woman also produces a lubricating secretion, unless the penis itself is slippery insertion may be awkward and painful for the woman. It is advisable, therefore, to apply a lubricant not only to the head of the penis, but to the whole of the body of the penis as well.

There are a number of chemical lubricants available, most containing a spermicide of one kind or another, a feature which the manufacturers push most in advertising their products. It provides, they say, an added protection.

But if you are using a perfectly fitting cap with a thoroughly reliable spermicide cream, you are well enough protected, and the spermicidal properties of the lubricant are not so outstanding a feature as to overcome the great disadvantage its use has, which is this. If love-play is to include penile caresses – as every love-encounter assuredly should – the chemical lubricant cannot be applied until the moment before the insertion of the penis; its pre-application would certainly rule out genital kisses, for there is no brand that is not unpleasant to taste and none that I know of that should be swallowed, even if the aversion to the taste could be overcome. But to take a tube, fumble with the cap, squeeze out a portion of the lubricant and smear it over the penis means a delay at the very moment when the rhythm of action and sensation should not be broken, a delay which could undo for the woman all the good she and her partner have achieved up to this point.

There is to hand, however, a natural lubricant whose properties no chemical can excel, and which also has the added advantage of costing nothing. It is saliva.

I have pointed out that during sexual excitement the salivary glands are extremely active. It takes only a couple of seconds after the man (or woman) has placed himself in position for insertion for either him (or his partner if the position adopted permits it) to transfer saliva, by means of the fingers, from the mouth to the penis. Not only is the rhythm not broken, but the touch of the penis with the hand will make quite certain that it is not, for the man at all events; and if the woman does it, her handling of the penis, by means of psychological association, will intensify her own sensations.

Second, and this is another fallacy I wish to explode, sleep is not an essential post-activity to orgasm. It is quite true that after the explosion of the tension built up during love-play there is an inescapable sensation of complete bodily relaxation and well-being brought about by the thoroughly satisfied sensory system. If the intercourse has taken place at the end of the day, sleep does come readily; but at other times it will be found that ten to fifteen minutes lying quietly will be quite sufficient for pulse and nerves to settle back to normal, and you will discover, on getting up, that, far from being tired, you will be full of energy and good spirits.

My third point also concerns post-orgasm. It is a good general rule that the couple should not separate until the penis has entirely subsided and the contractions of the vaginal walls have petered out. In fact, many women feel actual physical discomfort if the penis is withdrawn before it has become completely limp. The time which it takes this to happen not only varies from individual to individual, but from occasion to occasion in the same individual. But the man should follow the woman's wishes in this, and if she still feels the need of him after the penis has subsided he should remain where he is until a sign from her.

It will occur to you that some of the positions for coupling impose physical conditions in which retention of the position is tiring, and perhaps unnatural. From practically every position but one, however, it is possible, by exercising care, for a relaxed recumbent posture to be assumed. The greatest care must be taken that the penis does not leave the vagina while this is being done, but experimentation will quickly reveal the best method of reaching the required posture.

*   *   *

I wonder how many young women have asked themselves: 'Is it all right to have intercourse during menstruation?' The answer is, there is no medical reason why you should not. The only thing that may prevent it is your partner's unwillingness on aesthetic grounds. He will find, however, unless he is particularly fastidious, that he can quickly overcome his aesthetic objections if he is willing to try it once. Naturally, love-making at this time will preclude genital kissing by the man.

Many women who are 'slow starters' find that the moodiness and tension immediately preceding and during the first two days of menstruation can be rapidly dispelled by the fact that the vaginal contractions during orgasm have a similar effect upon the womb, which effect causes the flow to start sooner than it would naturally do. No physical damage can be caused by this.

Some women often experience desire that is so strong that although they may have a very intense orgasm – perhaps even two or three smaller ones before the big one – they still want to go on making love until they can come again. 'But my husband came when I did', they say. 'Is there anything we can do about it?'

It is curious how many otherwise sexually knowledgeable people are ignorant of the man's capacity for achieving orgasm. It is quite wrong to think that because the penis subsides after orgasm that is the end of it for the man until another day. Highly sexually active men know that this is not true; and it can be equally untrue for the average active man.

For some minutes after orgasm the head of the penis is excessively sensitive, and the slightest touch will cause pain of a kind that prevents erection rather than stimulates it. This condition lasts for ten minutes or a quarter of an hour or so, as a rule; and though the man cannot possibly be aroused during this time, thereafter erection can be promoted, though it will require physical stimulation and take some minutes to effect. But the resulting erection can be normally strong. Most men find, too, that the tempo of the sensations is much slower, so that it takes considerably longer to achieve orgasm, and consequently control of orgasm is much easier. The orgasm, when it does arrive, will almost certainly be very intense. Nor does this second orgasm necessarily mean the end. There is no reason why a normally healthy man should not experience three orgasms during as many hours, without suffering any ill or uncomfortable effects. By this time man and woman must have exceptional sexual appetites if they are not satisfied.

There are occasions, too, when many a man finds that though his orgasm has been intense, he is not completely satisfied by it. In such an event, the original erection is almost bound not to subside quickly, and may still be strong after the sensitiveness of the head of the penis has disappeared. If the couple have not separated, the man will quite naturally restore the erection by penile movements in the vagina. This is an occasion when he can perform penile movements for a considerable time without fear of orgasm; and it will be much to the liking of the woman. Under the influence of these movements it is possible that she may begin to experience erotic sensations before the man does. They will get out of step again, however, once the man has re-established his erotic sensations fully, and once he has done so he must apply stimulation either to the breasts or clitoris with the fingers, in order to increase his partner's tempo.

If, by a misjudgment, or because his sex-urge is so strong, he comes before his partner is anything like ready, the man should automatically accept the fact that a second orgasm is a must for him. He may have to pause for a minute or two, but there is scarcely any need for him to pause in stimulating his partner, though she will have to remain passive until his penis can again accept caresses without discomfort.

Yet another misconception is the idea that there are periods when the woman is incapable of being roused. If she feels she does not want to be touched, the cause is not physical but psychological, and though it may be a strong mood it can be overcome if only she will recognize it for what it is. If she will allow her partner to initiate love-play she will soon discover that she is as quickly roused as usual, and that the subsequent orgasm is just as pleasant and satisfying. She will also find that the mood has been completely dissipated. Nevertheless, there may be times when a woman does not need orgasm to achieve a sense of satisfaction and well-being.

You will now want to point out that I am contradicting everything I have been saying. I know that I have repeatedly emphasized that orgasm is as essential an outcome of inter-course for the woman as it is inescapable for the man, and that everything both of them do in love-play and coitus must be designed to bring this about.

Ninety-five times out of a hundred this is true, but I think you may have experienced certain occasions when your partner has approached you and you have felt that though you want him to have his own satisfaction, and even do not mind his caressing you, for some reason or other you are not eager to achieve orgasm. You will find that when the intercourse is over you are as relaxed and satisfied as if you had come.

Though I could not attempt to explain why this happens, you have no complaint. Curiously, though, your partner probably will have.

The sex-educators have done so good a job that most men nowadays not only appreciate the fact that their partners are as entitled to intercourse as they are, but feel that they have failed them if they do not bring them to orgasm at the conclusion of every intercourse. They consider the woman's failure to be a reflection on their own skill in making love, and on their manhood, since it does not appear to satisfy her.

Talk to your partner about this at some favourable moment. Explain to him that you are sometimes fully satisfied without coming. Promise him that you will quickly let him know if you must achieve orgasm and he does not appear to be helping you to it.

And now two points involving time.

*   *   *

It will have become apparent that love-making, if it is to be successful, must not be hurried. A question frequently asked is, how long should be allowed from the first approaches to orgasm? The only guide I am prepared to give is that the very minimum time required is twenty minutes, and this pre-supposes that the woman is quickly roused and reaches the point when she *desires* penetration in a quarter of an hour.

In this question of timing, as in almost every other aspect of love-making, 'how long' will vary from couple to couple and from occasion to occasion. The main thing to remember is that the aim of intercourse is to obtain the greatest relief from the sexual tension that is being experienced. In probably ninety-five cases out of a hundred this means that fore-play should not be hurried, that ample time should be devoted to it so that the quality of the orgasm achieved by both produces this complete relief for both. Experience will soon make clear how quickly the erotic sensory system responds, under certain psychological conditions, to this stimulus or that, to this tension or that.

If you find that you need an hour or even an hour and a half, you can be assured that there will be a host of others whose requirements are the same. If it is ever possible – and I do not see why occasionally it should not be – for you to devote two or three hours to your loving, I am quite certain that you will discover that the culminating experience will be outside anything the imagination has been able to conjure up. Similarly, what *proportion* of the total time should be devoted to love-play before penetration will vary from couple to couple, though much less frequently from occasion to occasion. There is no hard-and-fast rule, and you must decide for yourselves. As a general rule, however, if the love-play has continued until the woman desires penetration as the next essential step for her erotically, a maximum of seven to eight minutes for the achievement of orgasm, *after* penetration, can be taken as a good guide.

The next question is not how long, but how often. It is very surprising how many couples fear that if they make love every time they are physically urged to do so they may do themselves some harm, and they ask for guidance. First, let me say that there would have to be some mental instability or some physical defect present which would encourage either a man or a woman to make love in excess of their natural ability to do so, and thereby do themselves some physical harm.

I have already said a word or two about the frequency of the sex-urge, that accumulation of nervous tension and glandular secretions which sets in motion the sensory and subsequently the physical erotic apparatus. There are some who, as a direct result of their sex-urge, find daily intercourse essential to their well-being. For them this is not excessive. There is a small fraction whose urges are so active that they are sexually roused twice or three times daily. For them this is not excessive, provided they are otherwise healthy individuals. Three or four times a week is the general average, with the frequency tending to become less as one grows older.

The best guide is – make love as frequently as you are urged to want to by those promptings whose beginnings you cannot control. If you are indulging excessively, you will soon know. The vagina and penis will become painful with a dull nagging ache and a sensation of soreness, and a dragging sensation will throb in the small of your back. If these symptoms appear, avoid making love for a day or two. Acting with a kind of defence mechanism, the sexual urge will lie dormant while the symptoms persist, but intercourse may have taken on some of the characteristics of a habit, and without any natural sensation to prod you into a state of arousal you may deliberately bring on the initial sensations of arousal in yourself and your partner by artificial means, purely to satisfy your compulsion for intercourse at any cost. The sexual apparatus of both man and woman is so tough that it can be persuaded to respond to these artificial stimuli, which really have no relationship with love at all, but are the very near relations of lust.

However, as I say, *it will be very very rare indeed for the normal physical and mentally healthy couple* to make love to excess. If only they will keep an eye, so to speak, on the physical sensations of their urge to love, and make sure that it is sensations demanding satisfaction and not a psychological urge un-accompanied by the spontaneous physical sensations, they cannot go far wrong.

✻　　　　✻　　　　✻

This brings me to the end, within the limits I imposed upon myself when I was planning this book. I hope that, even if 'you knew all about it' beforehand, you will not decide that you have wasted your time reading what I have written. Perhaps some chance remark of mine will have cleared up a mystery, confirmed an uncertainty one way or the other, or perhaps set you thinking along some new line. If you 'knew some, but not all', I hope the new knowledge will help you.

Page.

53   The physical is the practical
means by which the intellectual is
achieved.

Page
111.   Second ½

Page.
113   Bottom of and 14 and 15

But whether experienced or learner, I wish you all joy in your partnership.

Index